IN MEMORY
OF THE MICHELIN EMPLOYEES
AND WORKMEN WHO DIED GLORIOUSLY
FOR THEIR COUNTRY

LILLE

BEFORE AND DURING THE WAR

Published by
MICHELIN & Cie
Clermont-Ferrand, France.

LILLE

ORIGIN AND CHIEF HISTORICAL EVENTS

The marvellous tales of "*Liliane*" and the forest rangers *Phinœrt* and *Lyderic*, which take Lille back to the days of Julius Cæsar, are mythical. The first mention of Lille in history dates back to the 11th century, when the town was divided into the "*castrum*" or entrenched camp of the Counts of Flanders (where Baudoin V. erected the Basilica and Forum in about 1050), and the "*forum*" (to-day the Grand' Place), where the church of St. Martin already existed.

The "*forum*" grew rapidly in the 12th century; the suburb of Fives, with its two churches of St. Saviour and St. Maurice, being enclosed within the new wall. There were no further changes of importance until the 17th century, when the Vauban fortifications to the north further enlarged the town. It was only in 1858 that Moulins, Vazemmes and Esquermes were included in the southern portion of the town, leaving the important suburbs of Fives and St. Maurice outside the ramparts.

Its situation on the frontier embroiled Lille in all the great wars. In 1213, *Philippe-August* took it twice from Count Ferrand, burning it completely the second time, to punish the inhabitants for having received their former chief. *Philippe le Bel* took it in 1297, and built the Château de Courtrai to commemorate the event. The *Flemish* conquered it in 1302, but were defeated in 1304 at Mons-en-Puelle by Philippe, who forced them to abandon the town after a month's siege. Then, for half-a-century, Lille belonged to the Kings of France, but the marriage of the Duke of Burgundy, *Philippe le Hardi*, with the Heiress of Flanders, in 1369, restored it to the counts. When *Maximilian of Austria* espoused Marie of Burgundy, daughter and Heir of Charles the Bold, last Duke of Burgundy, Lille became part of his dominions.

At the head of his armies, *Louis XIV.* besieged and took it in 1667 after "nine days of trench fighting," and the Treaty of Aix-la-Chapelle confirmed the capture.

As an advanced citadel, it defended the northern frontier, but in 1708, the *Spanish* were before its gates, and Marshal de Boufflers, after exhausting his supplies and ammunition, was obliged to surrender to Prince Eugène and the Duke of Marlborough. After a five years' occupation, the Treaty of Utrecht gave it back to France in 1713.

In 1792, it was besieged by 30,000 Austrians under *Albert of Saxe-Coburg*, who bombarded it day and night for nine days. The famous *Lille gunners* beat off the enemy, who raised the siege, and the Convention having decreed that "the town deserved well of the country," a commemorative column was erected in the Grand' Place (*p.* 26).

In the Franco-German War of 1870–1871, Lille remained outside the battle area, and the only local souvenir connected with that struggle was a visit from *M. Antonin Dubost* (now President of the French Senate) in October, 1870. Leaving Paris, which was besieged, in a balloon named "The Universal Republic," he landed between Rocroi and Mézières, going thence on foot to Belgium, and from there to Lille. He was received by the Commissary of the Government for National Defence (Mr. Testelin) (*p.* 50) and General Bourbaki, who had escaped from Metz, and harangued the people from the steps of the Grand' Garde (*Place de la Bourse*, *p.* 29).

In 1914, the victorious Germans were at its gates, and the Capital of Flanders was destined to suffer a four years' occupation.

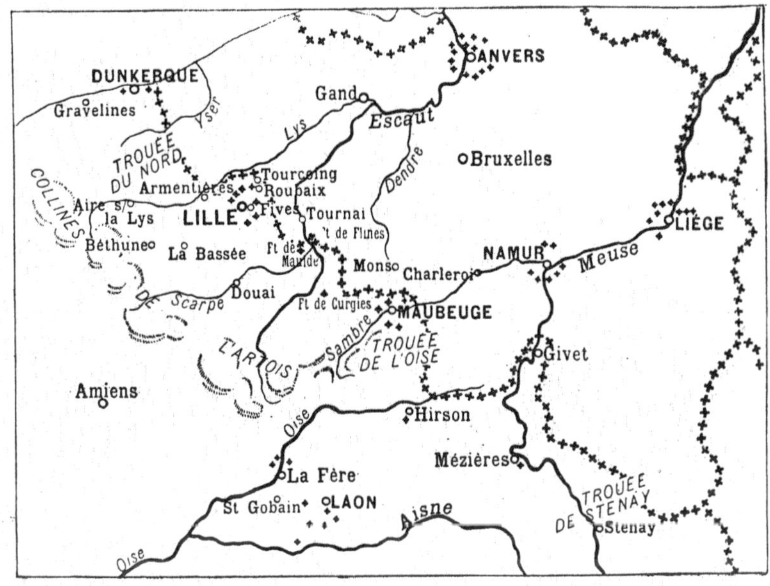

THE NORTHERN FRONTIER

LILLE AND THE GREAT WAR

Importance and Military Situation of Lille in 1914

Lying between the rivers Lys, Escaut and Scarpe, in the plain before the hills of Artois, Lille forms an isolated advance-post between *Maubeuge* (which guards the Pass of the Oise), and *Dunkirk* (which commands the region of the Dunes). *Vauban* had fortified the place, but the treaties of 1815 and 1871 deprived France of her essential points of support, and rendered these defences valueless. In 1873, *General Séré de Rivières*, Director of the Engineering Section at the Ministry of War, commenced a comprehensive scheme which aimed at the reorganization of the entire northern frontier, whereof Lille was one of the pivots.

Situated in the centre of France's richest coalfields and allied industries, Lille has justly been called "the Key to France's Treasure-House" (see "*Le secret de la frontière*," by M. Fernand Engerand, 1918). To enable it to withstand a surprise attack and hold out against a long siege, the city's intermediate defences were increased to such a degree that Lille became the point of support of the French frontier between the rivers Sambre and Lys. By thus protecting the Arsenal of Douai, it became possible to assemble a reserve army within the entrenched camp of Lille, 31 miles in length. The total cost of these works was 126,000,000 frs.

But, as in Vauban's days, a reactionary movement set in against defensive works, and it was demonstrated by their opponents that besieged towns must fall, and that in future the destinies of nations would be decided in the open battlefield. In 1880, the works of Séré de Rivières were abandoned.

NAPOLEON BRIDGE DESTROYED BY THE RETREATING GERMANS (*see p.* 52)

In the meantime, the great cities of the north, with Lille at their head, had become industrial centres of primary importance, thanks to their wealth of raw materials (coal, iron and steel). To protect them from the horrors of war, it was considered only necessary to make open towns of them. The fortifications of Lille were among the first to be condemned, as being of no real value, and a Bill to this effect was passed by Parliament.

Collaborators of Séré de Rivières gave the alarm in March, 1899, pointing out that the neutrality of Belgium was insufficient protection, that its violation was inevitable, that the Pass of the Oise was an open road for invasion, that with Lille outflanked, the Forest of Saint-Gobain (which Laon and La Fère, whose dismantling the Bill provided for, would no longer be able to protect) would fall, and that the enemy would be at the gates of Paris within a few days.

Finally, the fortifications of Lille were not dismantled, but were allowed to fall into disuse.

On the other hand, the eastern frontier was considerably strengthened. It was in vain that the *Belgian General Brialmont,* who had just completed the forts of Antwerp and Liege, pointed out that the abandonment of the northern frontier would inevitably cause a violation of Belgium's neutrality. Like her peaceful neighbour, France relied on the sacredness of treaties, and made it a point of honour to leave that part of her frontier practically unprotected.

At that time, Germany was neglecting the East, and making all her railways converge towards the Pass of the Oise. In other words, a frontal attack against the East being considered impracticable, Germany decided to turn it from the north. The fortifications of Lille were again condemned in November, 1911, and it is a curious coincidence that this was the year of the *Agadir Incident* and of the first tangible German threats of war.

In July, 1914, 3,000 artillery-men and nearly a third of the guns had been removed from the fortifications. On August 1st, the Governor, General Lebas, received orders to consider Lille an open town, but on August 21st his successor, General Herment, increased the garrison troops from 15,000 to 25,000, and later, to 28,000 men, taking units from each of the regiments in the 1st region. At this time, the armament consisted of 446 guns and 79,788 shells, to which were added 9,000,000 cartridges, 3,000 75 mm. shells and 12 47 mm. guns sent from Paris.

How Lille fell in 1914

(*See Maps on pages* 3 *and* 6)

At the beginning of the battle of Charleroi, *General d'Amade* was in the vicinity of Lille, with territorial divisions extending from *Dunkirk* to *Maubeuge*. The 82nd Division alone held the entire space between the Escaut and the Scarpe, with advance posts at Tournai and Lille. It was manifest that these troops were insufficient to offer serious resistance. However, the first care was to defend the town. For two days, trenches and shelters were made, and the troops sent to their respective positions.

On August 23rd, the British, defeated on the previous day at Mons, retreated, leaving Tournai unprotected. The Germans drove out the 82nd territorial Division and entered the town. Elsewhere, they advanced as far as Roubaix-Tourcoing, blowing up the station of Mouscron. The French territorials counter-attacked vigorously, and units of the 83rd and 84th regiments reoccupied Tournai during the night.

In the early morning of the 24th, *General de Villaret*, commanding the 170th Brigade, organized the defence of the bridges over the Escaut, where sharp fighting took place. However, his troops were obliged to fall back about noon, before the numerically superior enemy forces.

While these events were taking place close to Lille, the Mayor requested that the town should not be needlessly exposed to the horrors of a siege. A meeting of the principal civil authorities (town councillors and members of both Houses of Parliament) was held, at which it was decided to petition the Government to declare the town open, and withdraw the military. At 5 p.m. on the 24th, a telegram arrived from the War Minister, with orders to consider Lille undefended, and to evacuate the troops between La Bassée and Aire-sur-la-Lys.

On the 25th, the right wing of the German army was reported to be advancing, protected by about three divisions of cavalry with supporting artillery. Patrols reached the outskirts of the town soon afterwards.

General Herment executed the orders he had received. Moreover, he knew that the neighbouring town of Maubeuge was holding out with 45,000 men, and that the Belgian army was intact at Antwerp.

On September 2nd, enemy detachments entered Lille, disappearing three days later. The town was only occupied by patrols, who had orders to secure the German right (Von Kluck's army), which was executing its famous flanking movement. Then came the *Victory of the Marne*. After the German retreat and the indecisive *Battle of the Aisne*, the enemy began their northward movement known as the "Race for the Sea," the aim of which, on either side, was to turn the adversary's wing.

On October 3rd, Joffre joined the 10th army under *General de Maud'huy* to reinforce his left and prevent its envelopment. The 21st Army Corps arrived from Champagne, and the 13th Division detrained to the west of the town.

On the morning of the 4th, battalions of Chasseurs, belonging to the 13th Division, received orders to take up positions to the north and east of the town. After spending the night at Armentières, they passed through Lille, where they had an enthusiastic reception.

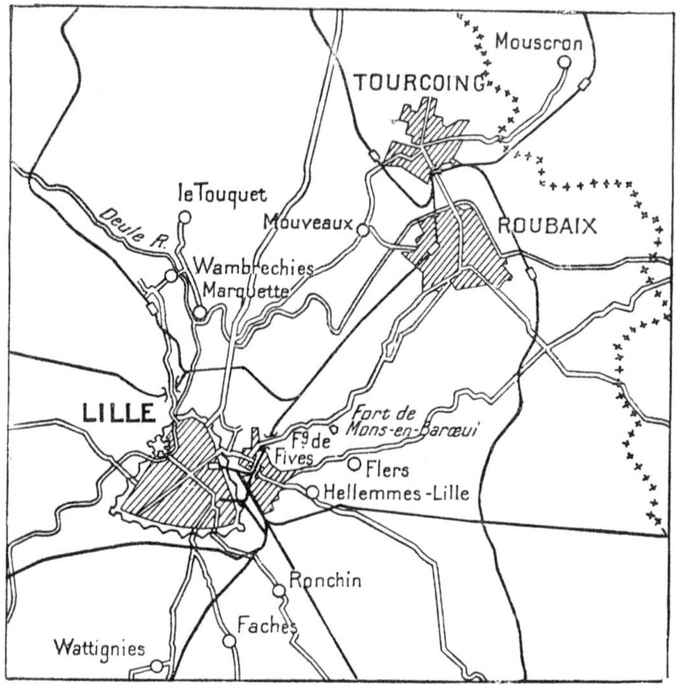

The 17th Battalion, which was to occupy the suburb of Fives, was met with a sharp fusillade as it left the ramparts. Organizing promptly, it drove the enemy from the railway station and fortifications, capturing a number of machine-guns and prisoners. To the north of the town, the French troops came into contact with German patrols near Wambrechies and Marquette, while the 7th cavalry Division had skirmishes in the neighbourhood of Fouquet.

Meanwhile, the garrison, consisting of territorials and Algerian mounted troops, took up positions to the south of Faches and Wattignies, in liaison, at Ronchin, with other units of the 13th Division. The enemy attacked at this point, and reached the railway.

On the 5th, after a sharp counter-attack, the French took Fives, Hellemmes, Flers, the Fort of Mons-en-Barœul and Ronchin. To the west of the town cavalry engagements took place along the Ypres Canal. On the 6th, the 13th Division left the outskirts of the town, following the 21st Corps in the direction of Artois. Only two battalions of Chasseurs were left in Lille.

On the 7th, the two battalions of Chasseurs rejoined the 13th Division, the defence of Lille being left to the territorials and Algerian troops. On the 9th and 10th, the 2nd cavalry Corps engaged the enemy near Estaires-Merville (between Aire-sur-la-Lys and Armentières), but was unable to open the road to Lille, which was then left to its fate.

At 10 a.m. on the 9th, the first enemy aeroplane appeared, and dropped two bombs on the General Post Office. In the afternoon, all men from 18 to 48 years of age were ordered to the Béthune Gate, with instructions to leave Lille immediately.

AFTER THE BOMBARDMENT: A FALLING HOUSE IN THE RUE DE PARIS

A crowd of people from Lille, Tourcoing, Roubaix and the neighbouring villages, left on foot for Dunkirk and Gravelines. Several died on the way of exhaustion, others being taken prisoners by the Uhlans. The last train left at day-break on the 10th. At 9 a.m., the first enemy shell burst, being followed by many others which fell in the neighbourhood of the station, and on the Prefecture and Palais des Beaux Arts. The afternoon was quiet, but at 9 a.m. the bombardment began again, lasting until 1 in the morning, then from 5 a.m. to 8 a.m. and from 10 a.m. to 6 p.m. On the 12th, when the garrison capitulated, 80 civilians had been killed and numerous buildings destroyed by the bombardment. That part of the town near the railway station was almost entirely destroyed (*see plan, p.* 25).

The Rue Faidherbe, Café Jean, Grand Hôtel, Grande Pharmacie de France, part of the Rue des Ponts-de-Comines, and the whole of the Rue du Vieux-Marché-aux-Poulets, were in ruins. The Hôtel Continental in the Parvis-St.-Maurice Square, was a mere heap of rubbish. The Rue de Béthune, Rue de l'Hôpital-Militaire and Rue du Molinel were partially destroyed. In the Boulevard de la Liberté, the premises of the "Belle Jardinière" Stores were wiped out (*p.* 38).

At 9 a.m., on October 13th, while hundreds of fires were still burning, five companies of Bavarian troops entered the town, followed throughout the day by Uhlans, Dragoons, Artillery, "Death Hussars" and Infantry. The occupation had begun.

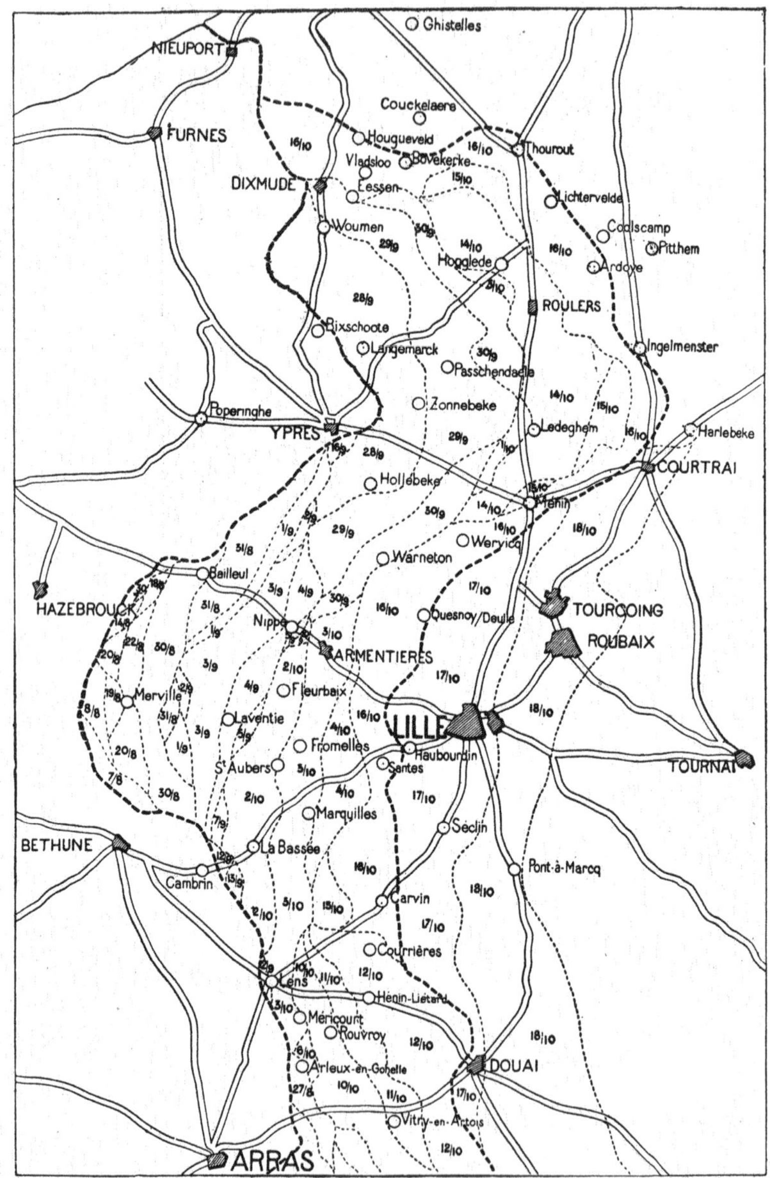

The Manœuvre of Marshal Foch

This map shows the successive advances of the Allies, from August 1st (1/8) *to October 18th* (18/10). *On October 16th* (16/10) *the line reached (shown by thick dots) threatened Lille with envelopment, and forced the enemy to retreat along a wide front.*

The Deliverance

For more than three years the inhabitants of Lille had heard the guns thundering almost at their gates, as for a long while the front was bounded by Armentières and Lens. In *December*, 1914, the Battle of Artois partially cleared Arras. The offensive of *May–June*, 1915, was marked by the capture of Notre-Dame-de-Lorette, Ablain-St.-Nazaire, Carency, Souchez, stopping at Vimy Ridge and hemming in Lens on the south. The victory of *September–October*, 1915, cleared Lens further to the north, by the capture of Loos. *In March*, 1918, a powerful German offensive from Armentières, forced the Allies back for several months, until the successive and correlated offensives of the Allies, under Foch, beginning on July 18th, finally liberated the French soil, town by town, and village by village. In August and September there was an advance along the whole front from the Argonne to the Artois, while in October, the Artois-Picardy front also burst into flames.

While the *French*, in the centre of their line of attack, crossed the Oise at Mont-d'Origny, to the south-west of Guise, the *British*, north of Douai and east of Lens, encircled Lille more closely on the south, and approached Séclin, Aubourdin and Quesnoy-sur-Deule.

At the other end of the front, on the left, *Belgian*, *British* and *French* forces under the *King of Belgium, Albert I.*, took the offensive, and on the 14th, 15th and 16th of October, in spite of the rain and mud, took Roulers and Thourout. Meanwhile, the 2nd British Army captured Menin, crossed the Lys 9 miles from Lille, taking from the rear the northern defences of the latter. In possession of Menin and Bouchain, the British continued to encircle Lille and Douai, and approached the two ends of the important Menin-Tourcoing-Roubaix-Cysoing-Orchies-Somain-Cambrai railway.

On the 14th, the Germans, who were preparing to evacuate Lille, destroyed the railway behind them, and on the 15th, burnt the goods station of St. Sauveur, after hurriedly plundering it.

At 4 a.m. on the 17th, the inhabitants were ordered to form up and march towards the British lines.

At 5 a.m. on the 17th the last of the Germans left Lille, after blowing up all the bridges and a number of locks on the canal.

At noon, on the 1,536th day of the war, the 5th British Army entered Lille, after a four years' occupation.

Although they had organized powerful defences to a depth of 12 miles around the town (barbed-wire entanglements, concrete trenches, etc.), the Germans made only a faint show of resistance. To console the people at home, the newspapers (*Strassburger Post*) announced that "*retreat was the only way to preserve the elasticity of the front and prevent a break-through at all costs.*" (See opposite, Map showing, step by step, the advance of the Allies, from August 1st to October 18th, 1918.)

The joy of the liberated population may best be expressed by the words with which the *Mayor of Lille* received *Président Poincaré* on October 21st: "*For four years we have been like miners buried alive, listening for the sound of the rescuers' picks; then all at once the dark gallery opens and we perceive the light.*"

In Paris, the news was received with singing and cheers. In the Place de la Concorde, the Statue of Lille was decorated with the French and British colours and flowers. The Fourth National Loan, named the "Liberation Loan," opened under the most favourable conditions.

FRENCH AND BRITISH PRISONERS
(Rue Faidherbe and Place du Théâtre, before the ruins of the Café Jean)

(Most of the photographs in the "Occupation of Lille" portion of this Guide, were taken by M. Hazebroucq, engineer, in spite of enemy prohibitions and threats.)

BRITISH TROOPS DEFILING IN THE RUE LÉON GAMBETTA, OCTOBER 21ST, 1918
(A portrait of the King of Belgium is seen in one of the shop windows)

THE KAISER IN MOTOR-CAR, IN THE PLACE CORMONTAIGNE

THE GERMAN OCCUPATION

The German occupation began on October 13th, 1914. From the 13th to the 28th of that month it was *Major-General Wahlschaffe* who directed the operations, levied the War Contributions and chose the hostages. His successor, *Artillery General Von Heinrich,* was appointed Governor on October 25th, and held the post until December 27th, 1916, when he was made Governor of Bucharest. *General Von Graevenitz* was Chief of the Kommandantur, which occupied the premises of the Credit du Nord bank in the Rue Jean Roisin.

THE KING OF BAVARIA AND THE KAISER IN THE PLACE DE LA GARE

The Hostages and War Contributions

Sixty hostages were chosen from among the most notable persons in the town, and included the Bishop (*Mgr. Charost*), the Prefect of the North (*M. Trépont*), *MM. Delory and Ghesquière*, Members of Parliament, the Mayor (*M. Delesalle*) and deputy mayors. In groups of ten they were made to spend the night in turns at the Citadelle (*photo, p.* 51).

From December 31st, they were required merely to sign a presence-sheet, but were later again forced to spend the whole of their time (day and night) in the Citadelle, this time in groups of five. Finally, they had to sign a presence-sheet each morning and evening until October 5th, 1915, when this formality was dispensed with, *i.e.* after the Census operations had been completed.

In November, 1914, began exorbitant exactions in the guise of **War Contributions.** On the 4th, Von Graevenitz demanded a million francs to be paid on the 10th ; then two millions on the 17th, and three millions on the 24th, in addition to the expense of feeding the troops, which alone amounted to 10,000 frs. daily. After much negotiating the Governor finally agreed first to give more time, then to reduce the amounts of the contributions.

To ensure an effective control, a very strict *census* of the population was taken on August 27th, 1915. Particulars of the persons in each house were constantly posted up, and after September 1st **identity-cards** with photographs were obligatory. To be found in the street or even standing on one's doorstep without this card, was punishable by fine (3 to 30 marks) or imprisonment (one to three days).

LILLE

CARTE D'IDENTITÉ

Nº de la carte d'identité
(Nº der Ausweiskarte).
Nº du certificat d'inscription 1314/c IV
(Nº der Wehrfähigenliste).
Nom et prénoms Jacquet Eugène
(Vor-und Zuname).
Né le 22 Septembre 1869
(Geboren am).
à Compiègne (Oise)
(In).
Profession Courtier
(Stand).
Domicile Lille
(Wohnort).
Rue Denis Godefroy, 1
(Strasse).

Cette carte est exclusivement personnelle. Elle ne donne droit à aucune prérogative (libre circulation, etc.).

Elle sera toujours portée par son propriétaire qui devra la présenter à toute réquisition.

Signature du possesseur :
(Nom et prénom).
(Unterschrift des Inhabers) :
(Vor-und Zuname).

PHOTOGRAPHIE

Cachet de la Mairie

SIGNALEMENT :
(Personalbeschreibung)
Taille (Grösse) 1m75
Cheveux (Haare) gris
Yeux (Augen) marrons
Nez (Nase) ordinaire
Barbe (Bart) grisonnante
Signes particuliers (Néant)
(Besond. Kennzeichen)

Diese Karte dient lediglich zum Ausweise des Inhabers, welcher sie stets bei sich tragen und auf Verlangen vorzeigen muss.

Signature de l'employé qui est responsable de l'exactitude du nom indiqué.
(Unterschrift des Angestellten).

M. JACQUET'S IDENTITY CARD (*see p.* 16).

Passes

DISTRIBUTING PASSES IN THE RUE JEAN-ROISIN (*see plan, p.* 25).

In January, 1915, the Kommandantur drew up rules for the granting of passes, a fruitful source of profit to the Germans, and of annoyance to the population. A scale of prices provided even for the shortest journeys. Funeral processions going to the South Cemetery were also required to have passes (free), to go through the Porte des Postes, and were escorted by soldiers, both going and coming, to prevent the people from leaving the ranks.

However, little by little, the people took up their occupations again. Forty schools for boys and girls re-opened early in November. Of the remainder, five had been destroyed, two turned into hospitals and ten into barracks. The higher schools and, later, the Lycée reopened, as did also the Conservatoire, whose pupils were exempted from having passes. The only newspapers allowed were the *Bruxellois* and the *Gazette des Ardennes*, both under German control. On November 15th, 1915, at the request of the Kommandantur, the Municipality started the bi-weekly *Bulletin de Lille*, which appeared on Thursdays and Sundays, and contained the Proclamations, Birth and Death notices, etc.

.EQUISITIONING EDDING IN .HE RUE RATISBONNE.

Next came the **Requisitions :** saddles and bridles, bicycles, photographic apparatus, telephones, bedding and horsehair (photo opposite). The Germans relentlessly seized all bedding, including that of the old people, some of whom died of cold from sleeping on

bare stone floors. Neither sickness nor old age could soften them, and when at last Lille was relieved, very few houses contained any bedding.

Famine

The town now began to be threatened with **famine.** Since 1914, bread had only contained one-third of wheat flour. At the request of the Military Authorities, the Mayor sent an **urgent appeal** to Switzerland for help, to save the women and children from starving, and cited the case of Strasburg generously revictualled by her in 1870. In March, 1915, a *Commission of Swiss Officers* visited Lille, but was unable to conclude arrangements. On April 19th, after lengthy negotiations, the *Comité National Belge*, under the patronage of the *Ambassadors of the United States and Spain,* obtained permission to revictual the famine-threatened town.

In the meantime, recourse was had to various expedients to eke out the stocks of food. In December, wheat flour was mixed with rye, Indian corn and rice. In April, potatoes were added. On the 11th, bread cards were inaugurated, fixing the daily ration per head at 9 oz. The inhabitants were divided into two classes, the ration being distributed every other day.

The gold, silver and copper coinage disappeared, and was replaced by cardboard pennies and paper " bons " (photos above and below).

THE KAISER AND THE KING OF BAVARIA IN FRONT OF THE RUINS IN THE RUE DE TOURNAI (PLACE DE LA GARE).

THE REIGN OF TERROR

Prohibitory Decrees followed in quick succession, in an endeavour to terrorize the people, who were forbidden to possess arms, approach the prisoners, import Belgian tobacco, or sell their wares in the streets, breaches being punished often with vindictive severity. Two of the first **victims** were the Prefect (*M. Trépont*) and his secretary (*M. Borromée*), the former accused of treason, the latter of stirring up revolt against the German Authorities. Their " crime " was that, on August 24th, in conformity with their duty, they had mobilized the French citizens, within sight of the enemy. They were roughly handled at the time by the German soldiers, and would probably have been shot, but for the intervention of one of the University professors (*M. Piquet*), who, acting as interpreter, managed to smooth matters over. After being closely watched and spied on, they were **arrested** on February 17th, 1915. M. Borromée was tried by Court-Martial on March 13th, and sent to **prison** at Alrath. Nine months later (December 27th, 1915), his release was obtained through diplomatic representations. The Prefect was sent as **hostage** first to Rastatt, then to Cellaschloss in Hanover, and his liberation was only obtained on January 17th, 1916.

In April, 1915, a system of Roll Calls was inaugurated, to prepare the way for the wholesale **deportations** which followed. At a given time and place, the people were required to present themselves, with a small quantity of baggage. Absentees were first fined, then imprisoned, the penalty increasing in severity with each succeeding " offence."

Domiciliary searches were carried out at all hours of the day and night, for hidden soldiers, arms, carrier-pigeons, smuggled French newspapers, and the like

Then, as if fines, imprisonment and starving were not punishment enough, the Germans started **shooting.**

AVIS

Les personnes mentionnées ci-dessous ont été condamnées par le Tribunal du Conseil de Guerre et fusillées ce même jour à la Citadelle, à savoir :

Le Marchand de Vins en Gros	Eugène JACQUET
Le Sous-Lieutenant	Ernest DECONINCK
Le Commerçant	Georges MAERTENS
L'Ouvrier	Sylvère VERHULST

1° Pour avoir caché l'aviateur anglais qui a atterri à Wattignies, le 11 Mars dernier, l'avoir hébergé et lui avoir facilité son passage en France, de sorte qu'il a pu rejoindre les lignes ennemies ;

2° Pour avoir entretenu et aidé des Membres des Armées ennemies et, après avoir quitté leur uniforme, séjourné dans Lille et les environs et les avoir fait évader en France.

Par proclamation du Gouverneur, du 7 Avril 1915, ces deux cas étant considérés comme espionnage, sont portés à la connaissance du public pour quils servent d'avertissement.

LE GOUVERNEUR

Lille, le 22 Septembre 1915.

NOTICE

The undermentioned persons were tried by Court-Martial and shot to-day at the Citadel:

Wholesale Wine merchant:	EUGÈNE JACQUET.
Second-Lieutenant:	ERNEST DECONINCK.
Shop-keeper:	GEORGES MAERTENS.
Workman:	SYLVÈRE VERHULST.

(1) For hiding the British aviator who landed at Wattignies on March 11 last, supplying him with food and lodging, and helping him to reach France and get back to the enemy lines.

(2) For assisting members of the enemy forces, helping them to remain in Lille and neighbourhood in civil dress and procuring their evasion to France.

In conformity with the Proclamation of the Governor, dated April 7, 1915, these two cases are considered as espionage, and are brought to the notice of the public as a warning.

Lille, September 22, 1915. THE GOVERNOR.

The Case of the Four

When, on October 12th, 1914, the small garrison which was holding Lille, surrendered, several hundred French soldiers escaped capture and hid themselves in the town. Until evasion should be possible, it was necessary to feed and shelter them, and this *M. Jacquet*, a wholesale wine merchant, undertook to do. A good organizer, his coolness and courage fitted him

Citadelle de Lille 22 Septembre 1915.

Ma bien chère femme,
Mes très chers enfants,

Au moment de partir pour le poteau d'execution, j'embrasse tendrement une dernière et suprême fois votre image adorée Mon dernier baiser déposé du fond de mon cœur ici pour vous. Adieu!

Ici mon Baiser – (x x x)

Vive La France! EJacquet

The Citadel, Lille, September 22, 1915.

My Beloved Wife and Children,

At the moment of starting for the place of execution, I tenderly embrace your dear image for the last time. My last kiss, from the bottom of my heart, here for you. Farewell! Long live France!

E. JACQUET.

---

well for the task. He was assisted by his daughter *Geneviève* (who, later, narrowly escaped being shot), his friends *Deconinck* and *Georges Maertens* and a Belgian, *Sylvère Verhulst*.

On March 11th, 1915, a British aviator was forced to land in the town, after having bombed a German telephone station. Hidden by Jacquet, he eventually escaped to Belgium, guided by Melle. Geneviève. A few days later, he again flew over the town and dropped notes reading as follows: "*Lieutenant Mapplebeck sends his compliments to the Kommandant of the German Forces in Lille, and regrets that he was unable to make his acquaintance during his recent pleasant stay in the neighbourhood.*"

The joy of the inhabitants and the rage of the Kommandantur may be better imagined than described in print. Orders were immediately given, and the "Polizei" set to watch. Previously, on March 16th, notices had been posted up all over the town, threatening with death any person who should hide "any member of the enemy forces."

Hostages, including the foremost persons in the town, were **imprisoned** in the Citadelle, while the liberties of all were severely curtailed. Passes to and from the surrounding villages were stopped, and "lights out" was sounded at 5 p.m.

Being unable to imprison the entire population, the Kommandant deprived them of **liberty** and **air** in mid-summer.

Meanwhile *Jacquet*, who knew that he was suspected, made light of the danger.

Arrested several times under various pretences, all efforts to incriminate him failed. However, a **spy** was at last found, who undertook to do the business. Passing himself off as a French prisoner, he asked Jacquet and his friends to help him, and then betrayed them to the "Polizei." A new

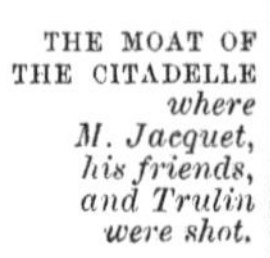

THE MOAT OF THE CITADELLE *where M. Jacquet, his friends, and Trulin were shot.*

search enabled the Germans to lay hands on 2,000 frs. in gold, but they could not find any incriminating documents (the list of the soldiers in hiding, 200 in number, was in the upholstering of an armchair at Deconinck's house).

In consequence of the spy's information, Deconinck's house was watched. Informed of the recent search of Jacquet's premises, Deconinck was looking round for a safer hiding-place, when his next-door neighbour, who was in the secret, suggested that the armchair would be safer in her keeping. The offer was well-meant but unfortunate, as the Police, who were on the watch, seized the chair, smashed it and found the list. Returning at once to Jacquet's house, they arrested him and his daughter, and locked them up in the Citadelle.

At the same time, Deconinck, Maertens and Verhulst were arrested.

Jacquet's daughter, Melle. Geneviève, owed her life to lack of evidence.

The four men were tried on September 16th and sentenced to death. They were shot on the morning of September 22nd, and died bravely, " standing, their hands free, and their eyes unbandaged." Their last words, shouted together, were : " Vive la France, Vive la République." Their names are inscribed on the Roll of Honour of the Army, and the *Journal Officiel* of December 8th, 1918, announced that the Légion d'Honneur had been conferred on M. Jacquet.

Execution of Léon Trulin

When the war broke out, Léon Trulin, a Belgian subject, aged 17, was living at Lille. Intensely patriotic by nature, he burned to serve his country against the hated invader. With the help of a few comrades, among whom were *Raymond Derain* and *Marcel Gotti*, he got together various documents and succeeded in bringing them to the Allies across the Dutch frontier. In 1915, he decided to go back to France and enlist in the Belgian Army, in company with his friend Derain. On October 3rd they arrived at the frontier. For three hours, in the dark, they burrowed under the "live" wire entanglements, when suddenly the alarm was given. Lights flared up, shots were fired, and Trulin and his companions were taken. The documents found on Trulin proved to be his death warrant. His friends Derain and Gotti were condemned to penal servitude for life.

On his way to the place of execution on November 8th, Trulin's nerve (he was 18) gave way for a moment, but recovering himself quickly, he walked to the post with a firm step, and so another name was added to the long list of the victims of Kaiserism.

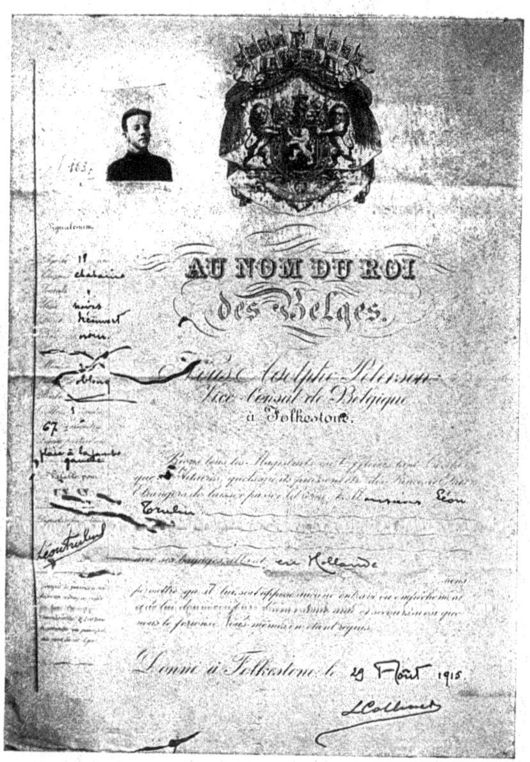

AU NOM DU ROI
des Belges.

Louis Adolphe Peterson
Vice Consul de Belgique
à Folkestone.

... Monsieur Léon Trulin ...

... en Hollande ...

Donné à Folkestone le 29 Août 1915.

L Collinet

TRULIN'S PASSPORT.

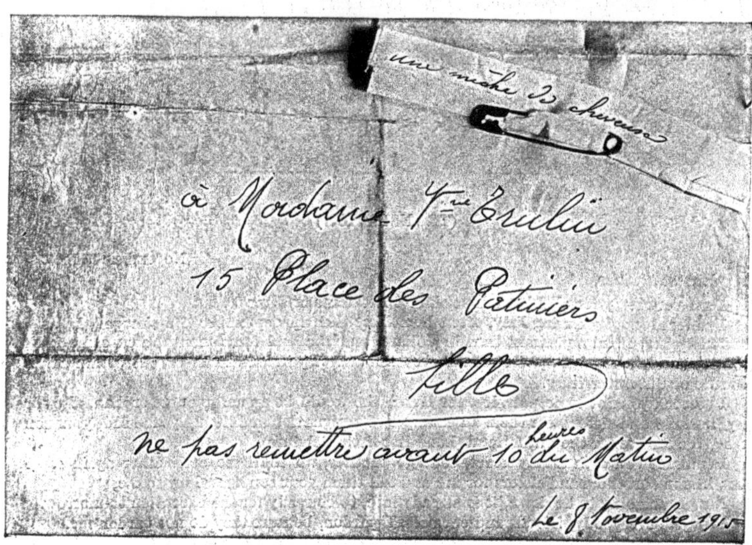

une mèche de cheveux

à Madame Vve Trulin
15 Place des Patiniers
Lille

ne pas remettre avant 10 heures du Matin

Le 8 Novembre 1915

TRULIN'S LAST LETTER TO HIS MOTHER (*pp.* 20, 21).

le 7 Novembre 1915

Ma bien Chère Mère

Je suis désolé de tout ce que j'ai fait depuis le 30 Juin, jour du départ.

J'ai bien souffert pendant le mois de Juillet souvent sans feu ni lieu, puis au mois de Septembre la vie a changée j'ai été un peu plus heureux, je me suis distrait en Hollande en Angleterre pendant 1 mois puis de retour en Belgique, puis crac voila le malheur. Je me fais prendre par malchance à ½ minute du territoire Hollandais.

Je vous en supplie ne désespérez pas et vivez pour René qui serai orphelin malheureux, vivez aussi pour mes frères et sœurs et montrez l'exemple de la résignation, et marchez la tête haute votre fils s'est dévoué pour sa patrie (Vive la petite Belgique.

Je vous embrasse bien fort et courage mère nous nous reverrons un jour, embrassez mes frères et sœurs pour moi et dites leur que votre fils a su mourir en brave.

Maintenant je vais me coucher il est déjà tard pour être près frais et dispos demain jour de l'exécution

Je pardonne à tout le monde amis et ennemis je fais grâce parce que l'on ne me la fait pas

(TRANSLATION)

November 7, 1915.

My dearest Mother,

I am very sorry for all I have done since I left home on June 30.

I suffered greatly during July, often homeless, then in September life changed, I was a little happier, I had a pleasant time in Holland and England for a month, then came back to Belgium, when suddenly misfortune overtook me. By ill luck I was caught within half a minute of Dutch territory.

I beseech you not to despair, live for René, who would be an unfortunate orphan, also for my brothers and sisters, set them an example of resignation and lift up your head, your son has given his life for the Fatherland (Long live little Belgium).

I embrace you with all my heart, courage, mother, we shall see each other again some day, kiss my brothers and sisters for me and tell them your son knew how to die.

Now I am going to lie down, it is already late, to be ready for the execution to-morrow.

I forgive everybody, friends and enemies, I pardon, because they do not pardon me.

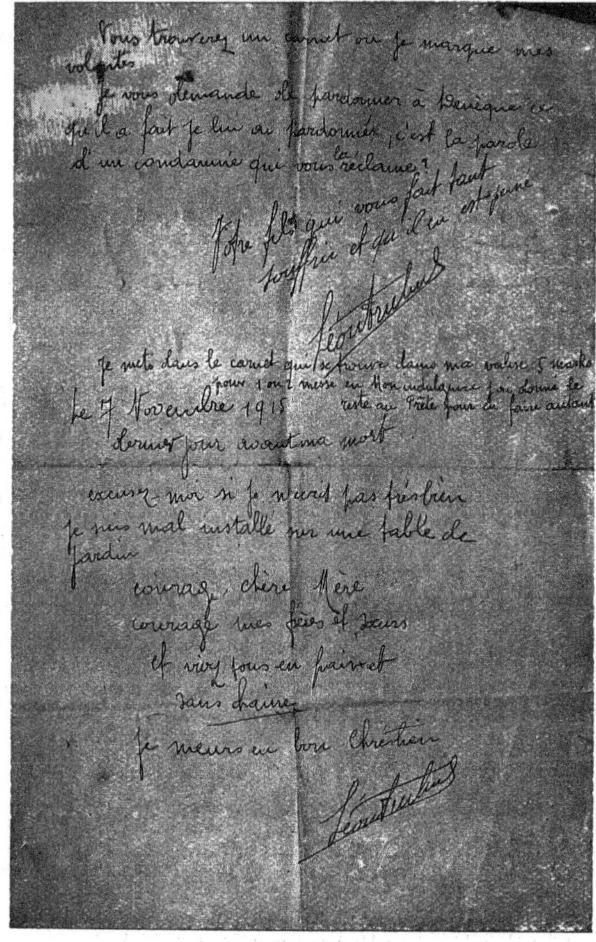

Vous trouverez un carnet où je marque mes volontés

Je vous demande de pardonner à Denèque ce qu'il a fait je lui ai pardonné, c'est la parole d'un condamné qui vous la réclame?

Votre fils qui vous fait tant souffrir et qui en est peiné

Léon Trulin

Je mets dans le carnet qui se trouve dans ma valise 5 marks pour 1 ou 2 messe en bon indulgence j'ai donné le reste au Prêtre pour en faire autant

Le 7 Novembre 1915 dernier jour avant ma mort

excusez moi si je n'écrit pas très bien je suis mal installé sur une table de jardin

courage chère Mère courage mes frères et sœurs et vivez tous en paix et sans haine

Je meurs en bon Chrétien

Léon Trulin

(TRANSLATION)

You will find a note-book, in which I have noted my last wishes.

I ask you to forgive Denèque for what he has done, I have forgiven him, it is the request a doomed man.

Your son, who causes you much suffering and is deeply grieved.

LÉON TRULIN.

I have put 5 marks in the note-book which is in my bag, for one or two masses and an lulgence, I have given the rest to the Priest for the same purpose.

November 7, 1915, the last day before my death.

Excuse me, if I do not write very well, I am writing on a garden table.

Courage, dear Mother, courage, brothers and sisters, live in peace, without hatred.

I die a good Christian.

LÉON TRULIN.

The Explosion of the "Dix-huit Ponts"

On January 11th, 1916, at about 2 o'clock in the morning, a terrific explosion shook the town, hurling huge stones and débris in all directions for a distance of several miles. An ammunition depot situated in the south-east portion of the ramparts, between the Gates of Valenciennes and Douai, about 400 yards distant from the railway station of St. Saviour, had blown up. It was an enormous underground vault, commonly known as the "Dix-huit Ponts," because of the 18 massive stone arches which formed the entrance.

It will probably never be known how many thousand shells and tons of explosives blew up, as the greatest secrecy was observed by the German Authorities. All the soldiers who were there were killed. The damage was tremendous, whole streets and numerous factories, including two large spinning-mills, were entirely destroyed.

"LILLE IN TEARS."

At the funeral, which took place on Saturday, January 15th, 1916, there were 108 coffins, but this figure does not include the numerous persons who were literally pulverized by the explosion. The noise of the latter was heard at *Breda* in *Holland*, nearly a hundred miles away, and houses as distant as the Rue Jeanne d'Arc, Place Philippe le Bon and Rue des Postes were destroyed by the flying stones. In general, the catastrophe was stoically borne by the inhabitants, one citizen remarking: "There were enough shells to have massacred whole regiments. Better we should mourn our dead, than the precious lives of so many of our soldiers."

One huge stone, weighing more than a ton, fell in the studio of the sculptor Deplechin (Rue de Douai), Director of the Ecole des Beaux-Arts, who carved the bas-relief "*Lille in Tears*" on it (*see Itinerary, p.* 36, *and photo above*).

The Deportations

In 1916, the prohibitions increased in number, the people being forbidden to leave their houses after 6 p.m., or before 7 a.m.; to criticise the news published by the authorities, to remain at their windows, or to stand on their doorsteps, under a penalty of 5 to 10 days' imprisonment. They were also forbidden to use the trams without a special permit. These measures paved the way for the **deportations** of April–May, 1916. During Easter week, under the pretence that the revictualling of the population was difficult, the Governor decided to deport the inhabitants of Lille, Tourcoing and Roubaix into the country, and make them cultivate the soil. Rumours to that effect had been rife for several days previously, but the people would not believe it. However, all doubts were cleared away on April 20th, when posters warned the people to hold themselves in readiness with about 70 lbs. of luggage. The 21st was a day of painful suspense. On the 22nd at 3 a.m., German soldiers hemmed in the Fives Quarter, and placed

THE HÔTEL-DE-VILLE BURNING *on the night of April* 24th, 1916.

achine-guns at the corners of the streets. House by house, street by ·eet, amid blows from the butt-ends of their rifles, the Germans forced the ople out of their houses. They were counted like cattle, and the number ecked with the sheet posted up on each house. Those who were to go, stly girls, were forcibly taken from their parents and led away between ed bayonets, then loaded into cattle-trucks and sent to an unknown c. Girls were taken from mothers and wives from husbands, with cold-oded indifference. It was in vain that the Mayor and the Bishop in-gnantly protested, the former to the Kommandantur and the latter from pulpit. Methodically, this abomination was perpetrated.

For ten days the people lived in mortal suspense, asking themselves if d when their turn would come.

On Easter-Sunday night, the 64th German Infantry Regiment surrounded Vauban Quarter, the horror of the scene being intensified by the Hôtel-Ville in flames.

Each night, until April 30th, 1,800 to 2,000 persons were wrested from ir homes.

Although greatly depressed, the deported people recovered their courage the trains left the station, and to the amazement of the Germans sang "*Marseillaise*" in a mighty chorus.

Twenty-five thousand persons, mostly women and children, were forcibly en from their homes and made to cultivate the soil, break stones, build dges, make sand-bags, turn shells, etc., their only food consisting of a le black "bread," nauseating soup and broken scraps of meat.

As soon as the French Government learned the facts, a Note was sent the Neutral Powers, protesting against these inhuman deportations, ich were ordered by *General Von Graevenitz*, and executed by the 64th antry Regiment, commanded by *Captain Himmel.*

Five months later, thanks to the intervention of the King of Spain, onso XIII., these unfortunate people were allowed to go back to their nes.

For several months in 1917 things went better, but in 1918, the German thorities recommenced deporting. A first batch of men and women s interned at Holzminden, while on another occasion the women were t to Holzminden and the men to Jewie, near Vilna (Lithuania). The icial Records, to which the reader is referred, contain full details of these uman crimes and of the abominable treatment to which the exiles were jected: privations of every kind, humiliation, torture and degrading upations.

On September 30th, 1918, the Kommandantur ordered the evacuation all males from 15 to 60 years of age, but the German soldiers carried out

QUET'S GRAVE
e East
netery.

their instructions in a half-hearted way, and many escaped. The approaching sound of the guns and the lax discipline of the soldiers announced the Allies' Great Victory and the coming deliverance to the war-weary people.

On October 17th, the British troops entered Lille.

The Ruined Industries of Northern France

Before the war, Northern France was one of the most flourishing industrial centres in the country.

The metallurgical firms of the North produced annually over a million tons of **steel,** representing nearly a quarter of the country's total production. This steel was transformed locally into finished articles. The exceedingly prosperous **textile** industry was carried on mainly at Tourcoing, Roubaix, Rheims and Sedan.

The **flax** industry was also concentrated around Armentières, Lille and Halluin.

The **cotton** mills of Roubaix, Tourcoing and Lille were extremely prosperous and important.

The following general figures give an idea of the industrial importance of this region, which contributed one-sixth of the country's total taxes. Before the war, the annual industrial production was estimated at 4,000,000,000 frs., of which the textile industries accounted for 2,500,000,000 frs.

RULIN'S GRAVE
the East
emetery.

The industries of Northern France have been **ruined,** not so much by the war, as by the systematic **pillaging** and **destructions** carried out by the Germans.

Official documents left behind in Brussels by the routed enemy brought to light the existence of two German Organizations: the **"Abbau Konzern"** and the **"Wumba Waffen und Munitions-Beschaffungs Anstalt."** The mission of the **former** was to cripple France industrially, by methodically destroying her factories and mills, while the **latter's** agreeable and profitable task was to sell stolen French machinery and tools to competitive German industrial concerns.

LILLE
SCALE:
0 500 1.000 M.
A. Church of St. Andrew.
B. Church of the Virgin.
C. Barracks.
D. Church of St. Catherine.
E. Church de la Treille.
F. New Stock Exchange.
G. Police Station.
H. Hotel de Ville.
Palais de Rihour.
J. Law Courts.
K. Old Stock Exchange.
L. Church of St. Maurice.
M. Sugar Market (Museum).
N. Palais Rameau.
O. Octrois.
P Prefecture.
R O. L. of Consolation.
S. Statue of Faidherbe.
T. Theatre.
U. University.
U'. Faculties.
V. Museum and Art Gallery.
X. Arts and Crafts School.
Z. Pasteur Institute.
GARE DE ST ANDRÉ
ST ANDRÉ
LA MADELEINE
PARC MONCEAU
HIPPODROME
CITADELLE
ESPLANADE
BOIS DE BOULOGNE
CIMETIÈRE DE L'EST
FAUBOURG DE ST MAURICE
CANTELEU
GARE
FAUBOURG DE FIVES
GARE AUX MARCHANDISES
R. de Cambrai
Boul. Louis XIV
Boul. de Strasbourg
Boul. d'Alsace
LOOS
FAUBOURG DES POSTES
CIMETIÈRE DU SUD
PLACES
1 Pl. St André
2 – St Martin
3 – du Théâtre
4 Grande Place
5 Pl. de la Gare
6 – Désiré Bouchée
7 – Madeleine Caulier
8 – de Strasbourg
9 – de la République
10 Square Ruault
11 Pl. Catinat
12 – Sébastopol
13 – Philippe Lebon
14 – Philippe de Girard
15 – Leroux de Fauquemont
16 – de Tourcoing
17 – de la Nouvelle Aventure
18 – Jeanne d'Arc
19 – Cormontaigne
20 – Guy de Dampierre
21 – Antoine Tacq
22 – Barthélemy Dorez
23 – Jacques Febvrier
24 – de Fernig
HOTELS
aa H de l'Europe
ab Grand Hôtel
ac. H de la Paix
Post Office. Telegraph. Telephone.

VISIT TO THE TOWN

To enable tourists to visit the town quickly and thoroughly, we have drawn 4 itineraries, each of which starts from and returns to the Grande Place.

1st Itinerary (pp. 25 to 35).—**The Centre of the Town. The Ruins in 1914.**

2nd Itinerary (pp. 36 to 48).—**From the Grande Place to the "Dix-huit Ponts." The Ruins in 1916.**

3rd Itinerary (pp. 49 to 54).—**From the Grande Place to the Citadelle.**

4th Itinerary (pp. 55 to 58).—**The Old Town.**

FIRST ITINERARY

Quarters destroyed by the bombardment of 1914 *:* **Rue de Paris, Rue de urnai, Rue Faidherbe,** etc.

Monuments seen on the way : **The "Bourse," Town Hall, Palais de our, St. Maurice's Church, Tournai Gate, Theatre, "New Bourse."**

Starting-point : The Grande Place.

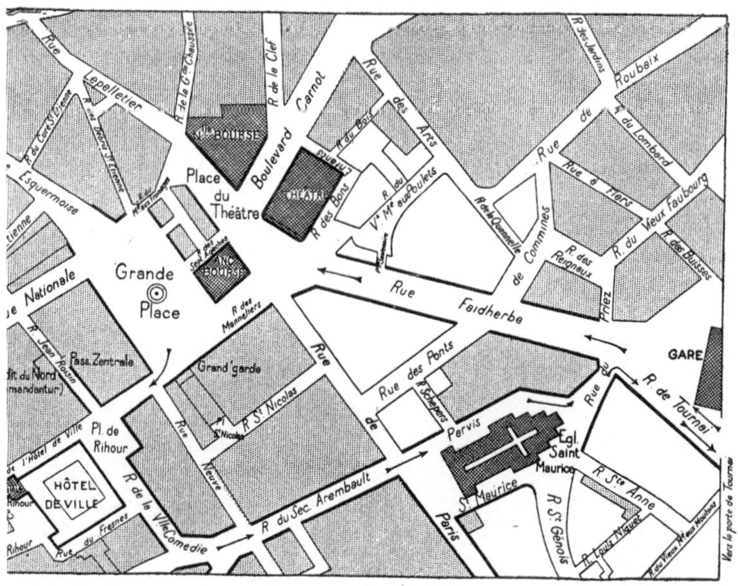

rting from the **Grande Place,** *follow the streets indicated by* **thick lines,** *in the direction of the* **arrows.**

The blocks of buildings shown by the blank spaces were destroyed by the 1914 *bombardment.*

THE OCCUPATION: PARADE OF GERMAN SOLDIERS IN THE GRANDE PLACE
Left: Column commemorating 1792; *right: Corner of the Bourse.*

The Grande Place

In the centre of the Square is a fluted Granite **Column** by *Benvignat*, erected in 1848 to commemorate the *Siege of Lille* in 1792. At the top is a **statue** of *Jeanne Maillotte* holding a lighted torch in her hand. During the siege of the town in 1792, she crossed the enemy lines and set fire to the Austrian batteries which were shelling the town. The name of this heroic woman was given to one of the streets, in which a later hero, M. Eugène Jacquet, lived (*see p.* 44). The inhabitants have surnamed the statue "*The Goddess.*"

THE DELIVERANCE: ENTRY OF THE 5TH BRITISH ARMY INTO LILLE
In front the "Goddess" statue (left) and the Theatre (behind the Bourse)

Behind the column is the **"Bourse"** or Stock Exchange. Square in shape, it stands between the Grande Place, Rue des Sept-Agaches, Place du Théâtre and Rue des Manneliers. Rising above the roof is a polygonal turret, the upper part of which forms a terrace with small timber-work campanile. It has been restored in recent times.

The "Bourse"

The Bourse is the finest specimen of 17th century Flemish architecture in France. Dissatisfied with transacting their business in the open, twenty-four merchants of Lille petitioned the King of Spain, Philippe IV., for permission to erect a building in the Place du Grand Marché, to be known as the "Bourse."

The plans of the architect *Julien Destré* were accepted in 1652. It was stipulated in the specification that the façades should be "of like symmetry and construction," that only the armorial bearings of the King were to appear over the entrances, and that the twenty-four buildings composing the edifice should be beneath one continuous roof, so as to form a harmonious whole. The petitioners were to guarantee the completion of the building within a given space of time.

To-day, shops on the ground-floor hide part of the façade, so that it is difficult to distinguish the bossages and semi-circular tympanums, but the rich, severe ornamentation of the upper stories, composed of caryatids, pilasters, pediments, and garlands carved in the stone-work, is plainly visible. The different periods of life (childhood, youth, and old-age) and the passions are depicted. The head of King Midas with stellated crown is especially noteworthy. A judicious use of brick with stone, while ensuring a harmonious *ensemble*, reposing to the view, also causes the relief motifs to stand out well.

THE INTERIOR COURT OF THE BOURSE, WITH STATUE OF NAPOLÉON I.

AN INTERIOR GALLERY OF THE BOURSE

Of the four doors ornamented with scroll-work, horns of plenty and royal coats of arms, in the four sides of the edifice, one gives access to the interior courtyard which is lined with four wide arcaded galleries. Doric columns of polished black stone support the vaulting, which is of brick, with binding ribs and nerves of white stone. On the plinth are heads of leopards connected by garlands of flowers and foliage. A bronze **statue** by Lemaire, representing Emperor *Napoleon I.*, protector of the national industries, stands in the middle of the courtyard. This statue was inaugurated in 1854, and was cast from old presses from the Mint of Lille, which had previously been made from guns taken at Austerlitz.

The interior galleries of the Bourse were decorated in 1850.

Facing each of the bays formed by the intercolumniations are large tablets of marble surrounded by carvings, which recall those of the façade. In the midst of this sculpture are the symbols of commerce, industry and science. Inscriptions recall the most important dates and institutions relating to the commerce and industry of Lille. The busts over them represent great inventors or learned men (Jacquart, Philippe de Girard, Chaptal, Brongniart, Chevreul).

On leaving the Bourse, cross the square to the left, and enter the Place de Rihour.

At the corner of the Grand Place, the black façade of the **Grand' Garde** decorated with trophies and curved pediments bearing the arms of France and Lille, should be noticed. A large shell-hole in the left-hand pediment has been temporarily bricked up.

Cross the ruins of the **Hôtel de Ville,** burnt down on April 24th 1916 (*photo below*), at the time of the deportations. To the right, abutting on the Hôtel de Ville, is the **Palais de Rihour** which escaped damage from the fire.

THE HOTEL DE VILLE, BURNT DOWN ON THE NIGHT OF APRIL 24, 1916 (*see p.* 23)

THE PALAIS DE RIHOUR AND THE RUINS OF THE HÔTEL DE VILLE

The Palais de Rihour

Built in 1457–1462, this palace was the residence of *Philippe le Bon*, Duke of Burgundy. Only an octagonal turret, the guard-room and the chapel of brick and white stone remain. The Hôtel de Ville was erected on its site.

The low guard-room, in which the town records are kept, is divided in the middle by three polygonal columns unequally interspaced. The stone staircase with ribbed vaulting and graceful ornamentation, was formerly the grand staircase. Transferred to its present position, it now leads to the chapel known as the "Salle du Conclave," where the magistrates of Lille sat until 1789.

To the right of the chapel is a brick building, the façade of which is divided by two similar gables. Jutting out at the corner is an octagonal turret containing two small vaulted chambers. Above is a third room with timber-work ceiling, known as the "Oratory of the Duchess." An opening in the wall communicates with the chapel, and through it the choir is visible. From this room, which is reached by a spiral staircase of stone inside the turret, it is possible to hear the service without being seen.

Re-cross the Hôtel de Ville ruins and return to the Place de Rihour. Follow

THE RUE DE PARIS: *in the background:* THE THEATRE *and* THE NEW BOURSE

the Rue de la Vieille-Comédie and Rue du Sec-Arembault (plan, p. 25); the latter comes out into the Rue de Paris, in front of **St. Maurice's church.**

ST. MAURICE'S CHURCH

The Church of St. Maurice
(*historical monument*)

The church was seriously damaged by the bombardment of October 1914, which set fire to the roof.

It is a curious specimen of the 15th century Gothic-Flamboyant style of Walloon-Flanders, and comprises five naves of equal height arranged quincuncially, whereas most of the churches belonging to that period have three naves under a single roof, the aisles being shorter than the great nave, while the tower is necessarily placed over the main entrance (*see St. Catherine's Church, p.* 54).

It also contains an ambulatory and an apse formed by polygonal chapels.

The façade, with its three portals, steeples of open construction, and white stone tower at the entrance, dates from the second half of the 19th century. The old square tower was pulled down in 1826 as unsafe. These different alterations were carried out under the direction of the architect *Lannissie.* According to *Monseigneur Dehaisnes,* the remarkable exterior of this church is due to these successive restorations and alterations.

ST. MAURICE'S CHURCH: THE NAVE

Inside the church are rows of round slender columns with sculptured capitals, irregularly spaced.

The springing of the binding ribs or projecting arches which line the vaults, and their graceful arched branches, rest on and meet at the capitals. The point of intersection of the arches is marked by a pendant keystone. High and broad mullioned windows (note the stone uprights dividing the bays) amply light the interior. In the choir aisles are the following **paintings:** St. Charles Borromée and St. Francis, by *Van Oost,* and "Les Disciples d'Emmaüs," by *Van der Burgh*; in the chapel of St. Barbara: "Vision de Ste. Therese," by

DOOR OF THE VESTRY

Van Oost and a landscape by *Van der Burgh*; in the chapel of the Virgin: "Mariage de la Vierge," by *Wamps*, "Glorification de la Vierge," by *Van Minne*, and "La Cène," by *Van Audenaerde*. In the vestry are 15th and 16th century **chasubles** and 17th century **tapestries.**

CHEVET OF ST. MAURICE'S CHURCH

THE RUE DU PARVIS-SAINT-MAURICE (*see plan, p. 25*)
(The photographer, with his back to the Church, faced the Rue Scheipers. In the background are the Theatre and the Campanile of the Nouvelle Bourse.)

After visiting the Church, take the Rue du Priez, behind the Church, leading to the Place de la Gare.

THE RUE DES PONTS DE COMINES (*see plan, p. 25*)
The operator faced the Rue Scheipers. In the background is the Church of St. Maurice, against which he had his back when taking the preceding photograph.

THE STATION AND RUE DE TOURNAI (*see p.* 15)

Follow the Rue de Tournai, on the right (numerous houses damaged by shells) as *far as the* **Tournai Gate.**

THE TOURNAI GATE

A temporary road replaces the bridge over the moat, destroyed by the retreating Germans.

RUINS IN THE RUE FAIDHERBE
View taken from the Place du Théâtre. In the background, the station.

The **Tournai Gate** was built in the reign of Louis XVI.

The **bridge** over the moats of the ramparts, which the Germans blew up before leaving, has been temporarily repaired.

Return by the Rue de Tournai and the Rue Faidherbe (partially in ruins) *as far as the Place du Théâtre: see the* **Nouvelle Bourse** surmounted by a tower, and the **New Theatre,** inaugurated during the German occupation.

RUINS IN THE RUE DE TOURNAI.

RUINS IN THE RUE DES ARTS.

SECOND ITINERARY

Starting from the **Grande Place,** *follow the streets indicated by* **continuous black lines,** *in the direction of the* **arrows.**

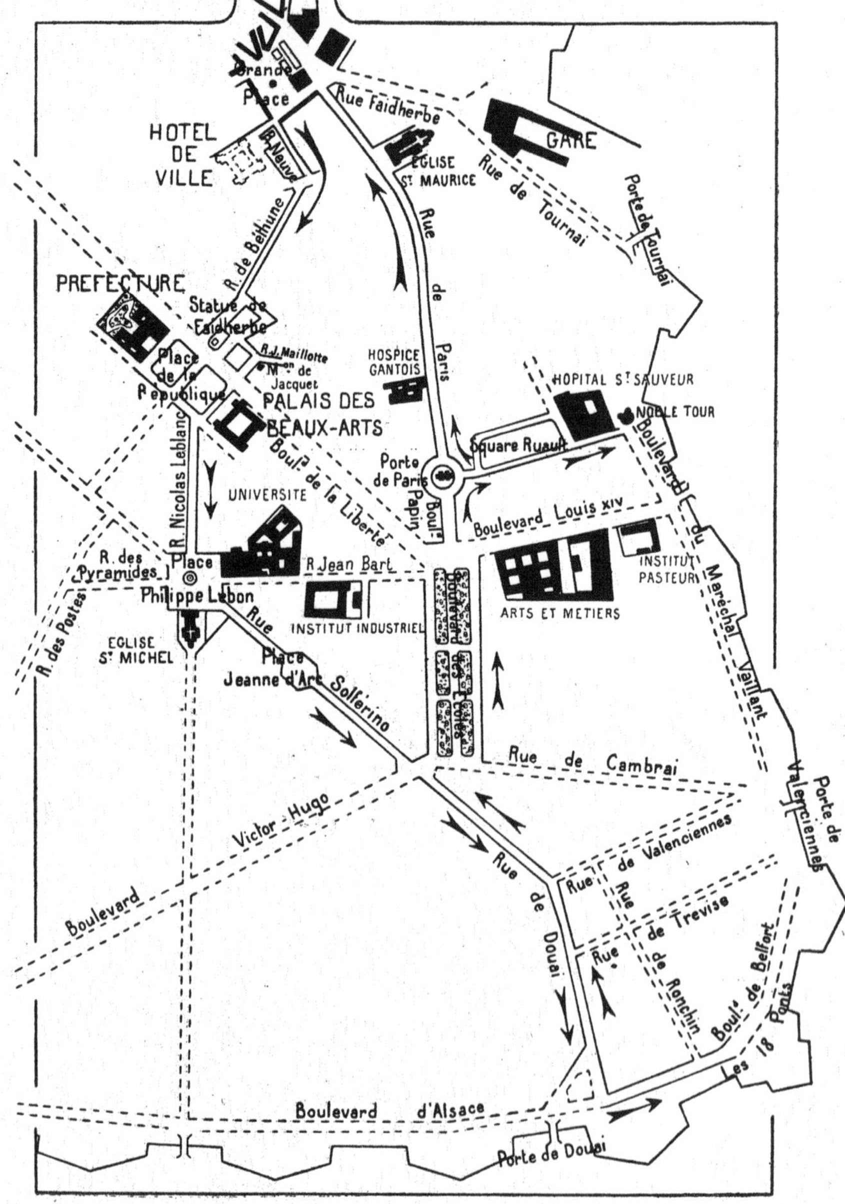

RUINS IN THE RUE DE BÉTHUNE

SECOND ITINERARY

From the Grande Place to the Douai Gate quarter, destroyed by the Explosion of the "18 Ponts."

Principal sights on the way : **The Prefecture, Museum** *and* **Paris Gate.**

Starting Point : **The Grande Place.**

To the right of the Grand' Garde, take the Rue Neuve, continued by the Rue de Béthune (one of those which suffered most from the bombardments).

Follow this street to the Place de Béthune and to the Place Richebé ; see the bronze equestrian **Statue** of *General Faidherbe* (1896), at the foot of which are two feminine figures with palm-branches and arms symbolising France and Lille. Two **bas-reliefs** representing the battles of Pont-Noyelles and Bapaume adorn the sides. The Monument is the combined work of the architect *Pugol* and the sculptor *Mercié.*

In front of the statue : Boulevard de la Liberté and the fine Place de la République ; *on the right* is the **Prefecture,** *on the left,* the **Palais des Beaux Arts.**

The **Prefecture** is a richly ornamented building, erected in 1869 from

THE PREFECTURE, PLACE DE LA RÉPUBLIQUE

THE PALAIS DES BEAUX-ARTS.

the plans of the architect *Matteau*. The walls have been deeply scarred in places by shell splinters (*note the white patches on the blackened facade*).

The **Palais des Beaux-Arts** was inaugurated in 1892.

Composite in style, it is very richly ornamented. Flanked by two round pavilions with cupolas containing staircases, its principal façade is in the Rue de la République. The **Museum of Lille** is installed there.

THE MUSEUM OF LILLE

This is one of the finest provincial museums in France. As early as 1795 it contained 183 works of art. A Consular Decree, dated the 14th Fructidor, Year IX, added 46 paintings taken from the collections of the Louvre and Versailles. The first catalogue, dated 1850, comprised 274 works of art, which number had increased to 1,275 at the time of the inventory of January 1st, 1908.

The Museum during the War

The Museum was the edifice which most suffered from the German bombardments. On October 11th, 1914, it was struck by 75 shells. The curator took measures at once to have the roof repaired and protect the collections.

However, the Museum was not proof against German greed. On Saturday, November 17th, two officers, accompanied by military policemen, came to "requisition" the works of art, in the name of the German authorities. After visiting the different rooms, and being unable to obtain the keys of the cabinets, they broke open the latter and took all the medals and miniatures, which they placed in paper bags from a neighbouring grocer's shop. The curator protested the same day, both verbally and in writing, to the Kommandantur and Military Governor.

THE BELLE JARDINIÈRE, *near the Museum (Boulevard de la Liberté).*

The miniatures were brought back on November 19th, and the medals on December 3rd, less various antique gold jewels, two miniatures, and two gold medals, which had been "lost."

Later, two well-known German art experts *Herr Demmler* and *Herr Professor Klemen,* armed with carefully annotated catalogues, made a general "requisition" comprising: 1,500 drawings (including those by Raphael and Michael Angelo), 420 paintings and 518 other works of art, all of which were packed up, labelled and sent off. The famous **"Wax Head"** (*page* 43) had, however, been hidden away in an underground vault, and replaced by a copy.

In an endeavour to justify their action, the Germans sent out a radiogram on November 4th, 1918, stating that the Museum of Lille had been damaged so seriously as to be unsafe for works of art, and that at the request of the curator, an inventory of the collections had been made and the latter transferred first to Valenciennes and then to the Old Museum in Brussels.

VISIT TO THE MUSEUM

The collections are classed under four distinct heads : **paintings, modern sculpture, archeological and lapidary specimens** and the **Wicar collections.**

I.—Paintings

The **Flemish** and **French** schools are the best represented. (*For a detailed description of the paintings, see* "*La peinture au Musée de Lille,*" *by François Benoit,* 3 vols *in* 4*to, with reproductions,* 1908).

The **Spanish** school includes a St. Jerome, by *Ribera,* dated 1643.

THE MARTYRDOM OF ST. GEORGE, *by Veronese* (*Cliché LL.*)

The **Italian** school contains The Martyrdom of St. George by *Veronese* (duplicate of the painting by *San Giorgis Maggiore* at Verona) ; two circular panels : Eloquence and Science (symbolized by two Venetian women with auburn hair), also by Veronese ; The Flight into Egypt by *Carlo Saraceni,* and the Assumption of the Virgin by *Piazzetta* (two very original painters little known in France) ; a delicate "Virgin with wild roses," of exquisite colouring, by *Ridolfo Ghirlandajo ;* "Magdalene at the feet of Christ" and a "Judith and Holopherne" by *Lambert Zustris* (often called Lambert Lambard)—two paintings of limpid colouring ; (note the delicate lilac-grey tints).

As befits the "Capital of Flanders," the **Flemish** and **Dutch** Schools of the North are fully represented.

The Mystic Press, by *Jean Bellegambe ;* the triptych, Virgin surrounded by Angels, attributed to *Gerard David ;* the first portrait of Philippe le Bon,

THE DESCENT FROM THE CROSS, *by Rubens* (*Cliché LL.*)

attributed to *Pierre Etret*; the Symbolical Fountain, an exceedingly fine altar-screen panel by *Thierry Bouts* de Haarlem, is particularly noteworthy; a portrait of Emperor Charles Quint at the age of 32, by *Christophe Amberger* and Charles Quint taking the Monk's Gown, by *Nicolas Francken the Elder*. *Rubens* is represented by seven paintings: The Descent from the Cross, of admirable clearness; the expression is more natural than that of the painting in Antwerp; Vision of the Virgin appearing to St. Francis, of warm colouring; St. Bonaventure Meditating, and St. Francis receiving the Stigmas (two fine long panels); The Death of Magdalene (a somewhat monotonous but strangely intense monochrome). *Van Dyck* is well represented by the following: The Crucifixion, considered by Paul de St. Victor to be his greatest masterpiece (the figure of Christ stands out clearly against a cloudy sky pierced by lightning); Portraits of an Old Lady and Marie de Médicis (in the background are seen Antwerp and the Escaut). The following artists are also represented: *Jordaens*, by the Prodigal Son, Christ and the Pharisees, the Temptation, and a wonderful study of cows; *Gaspard de Crayer*, by Martyrs buried alive (fine harmonious composition); *F. Franchoys*, by a Portrait of the Prior of the Abbey of Tongerloo, Gisherts Mutsarts, dated 1645. (Paintings by this artist are exceedingly rare). *Verspronck*, by the Portrait of Young Boy; *Jansen*

PORTRAIT OF OLD LADY

by van Dyck (*Cliché LL.*)

BOY'S PORTRAIT

by Verspronck (*Cliché LL.*)

Van Ceulen, by a very fine portrait of Anne Marie de Schurmann; *Pieter Codde*, by Conversation, of delightful colouring.

The **French** school, although incomplete (*Prudhon*, *Ingres* and *Antoine Watteau* are not represented), is nevertheless rich and instructive. First of all an *anonymous* 17th century Portrait of an Architect, whose pale harsh face arrests the attention and haunts the memory. *Ph. de Champaigne* is represented by the Good Shepherd; *Restout* by a Jesus at Emmaüs; *Mignard*, by A Judgment by Midas; *Largillière*, by a very fine portrait of his father-in-law, the painter, John Forest; *Douvé* (native of Lille), by a fine portrait of the painter Savage; *Jean Voilles*, by a delightful portrait of Madame Liénard; *François Watteau* (grand nephew of Antoine Watteau), by two amusing sketches: Procession of our Lady of the Vine in 1789 and The Old Clothes Market of Lille; *David*, by his first picture after returning from Rome, "Bélisaire" (1781), of which there is a reduced copy in the Louvre (this painting marks the re-birth of the antique); *Boilly*, a native of the district of Lille, is fully represented by his Triumph of Marat—master-

THE TRIUMPH OF MARAT, *by Boilly* (*Cliché LL.*)

piece of great truth and delicacy—and 28 portraits of artists painted for the picture "Réunion d'artistes dans l'atelier d'Isabey." The following are the names of these portraits: *Van Dael*, flower painter; *Houdon*, sculptor (grey overcoat); *Chaudet*, sculptor (seated); *Duplessis Berteaux*, designer (head resting on hands); *Hoffman*, art critic (long powdered hair); *Redoute*, flower painter; *Bourgeois*, designer; *Demarne*, painter; *Thibaut*, architect; *Swibach*, genre painter; *Lemot*, sculptor; *Serangeli*, historical painter (half-length, hands in pockets); *Taunay*, landscape painter; *Isabey* (red coat); *Percier*, architect (looking at a plan); *Talma*, actor; *Drolling*, portrait-painter (red waistcoat); *Corbet*, sculptor (grey coat and white waistcoat); *Meynier*, painter; *Fontaine*, architect; *Blot*, engraver; *Bidault*, painter; *Boilly-Chenard*, singer; *Girodet-Trioson*, *Gerard* and the remarkable group *Lethière* and *Carle Vernet*.

In the **modern** school, the following are especially noteworthy: La Médée, by *Eugène Delacroix* (strikingly dramatic), L'aprés-diner à Ornans, by *Courbet*, the colouring of which is unfortunately fading; La Becquée, charming genre painting by *Millet*; Effet du Matin, by *Corot*, remarkable for its beautiful effects of silvery light.

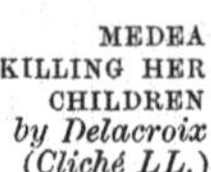
MEDEA KILLING HER CHILDREN *by Delacroix* (*Cliché LL.*)

II.—Sculpture

Of the collections of sculpture, only the fine **bust** of Bonaparte by *Corbet*, dated 1799, is worthy of special mention.

III.—Archeological and Lapidary Museum

The Archeological Museum contains the following remarkable works of art: Three 14th century **statuettes** of the Virgin (two of wood, one of marble); an ivory **diptych** of the Crucifixion; a 13th century **reliquary cross** of Flemish origin; divers curious specimens of **brass-work,** including the Censer of Lille, rightly considered a masterpiece; a richly embroidered **altar-cloth,** representing the Annunciation.

IV.—The Wicar Collections

The important Wicar Collections were bequeathed by the Lille painter, *Jean Baptist Wicar*, pupil of David (1762-1834), who in 1815 succeeded in protecting the Museum of Lille from spoliation by the Allies.

Commissary to Bonaparte in Italy, and later Director of the Royal Academy at Naples, Wicar adopted Roman nationality, and collected a large number of fine drawings and art treasures. Parts of his collections are to-day at Oxford. The famous "Wax Head" (*p.* 43) is in the centre of the Wicar Room.

There are several **Renaissance bronzes** worthy of note, also a **marble bas-relief** by Donatello, representing the Beheading of John the Baptist, and a fine terra-cotta **Head of Child** by Verrochio. The drawings merit careful inspection. The following are especially remarkable: Studies on pink and yellow grounds, by *Filippo Lippi*, *Filippino*, *Chirlandajo*, and *La Verrochio;* Head of Bald Man, by *Montegna;* 14 drawings on parchment, representing scenes from the Metamorphoses, Children's Games and Arabesques, attributed by L. Gonse to *Jacopo Francia*, attest marvellous delicacy and skill; two sheets of caricatures by *Leonard de Vinci* and 60 sketches by *Raphael;* studies in black and red by *Michaël Angelo*, especially a Dead Christ, figure of a naked man, fantastic masks and a series of 184 architectural drawings, generally known as the "Book of Michael Angelo." *Annibal Carrache*, *Le Guide*, *Guerchin*, *Sodoma* and *André del Sarto* are also well represented.

On the other hand, French drawings are few in number, the most remarkable being one by *David* for his "Serment des Horaces." The others include: "Le Corps de Garde," by *Boilly* (fine, carefully-finished drawing); a naked Woman, by *Watteau;* two drawings by *Ingres* for his "Apotheose d'Homère;" a drawing by *Poussin* for the "Massacre des Innocents"; a wonderful Portrait of Old Man, by *Lagneau*, an artist little known in the reign of Louis XIII, but a great master; lastly a fascinating fusain drawing by *Millet:* "Le Troupeau de Moutons au milieu d'un bois."

The "Wax Head"

The most celebrated work of art in the collections is the **Wax Head** (Tête de Cire), which has so often been reproduced in engravings, photographs and casts. This funeral souvenir, which stands in a golden niche in the middle of a room draped with red plush, was made to perpetuate the memory of a young girl 15 to 18 years of age. The pedestal and draperies are of terra-cotta, and date from the 18th century.

Of Italian origin, the head is attributed by some to Raphael, by others to Leonard de Vinci. The possibility of its being antique is no longer admitted. According to Gonse, it came from the Tuscan studio of Orsino Benitendi, and dates from about 1480. The wax was tinted at a later date.

THE WAX HEAD (*Cliché LL.*)

Leaning to one side, the face is pensive in expression. The neck is flexible and sits with easy grace on the shoulders. The cheeks are rather broad and somewhat flat, the chin round and short. A faint smile hovers round the delicate mouth. The eyes are considered by some to be rather small. The waving hair is divided into two graceful masses, which are rolled up on the back of the neck.

The expression of the face is enigmatical and changes with the angle from which it is regarded. Psychologists and artists alike will long discuss its charms.

When the two German experts *Herr Demmler* and *Herr Professor Klemen* " requisitioned " the collections of the Museum (*p.* 39), what they took away was a *copy* of this head, the original having been hidden in one of the underground vaults. It narrowly escaped destruction in October, 1918, when the Germans, previous to evacuating the town, cut the water-mains, so that the sub-basement of the Museum was flooded. Fortunately, the water did not rise high enough to do serious damage, and the head was eventually restored intact to its velvet pedestal.

Near the Museum, at the corner of the Rue Jeanne Maillotte and the Rue

Denis Godefroy which opens on the Boulevard de la Liberté, in line with the Museum), is the house where M. Eugène **Jacquet** lived (*his apartment was on the* 1*st floor, see photograph below and page* 16).

Leave the Place de la République by the Rue Nicolas Leblanc (*at the corner of the Square, by the side of the Museum*) *at the end of which is the* **Church of St. Michael.** *Continue as far as the Place Philippe le Bon: in the middle,* **Monument to Pasteur;** *on the left,* **University of Lille.**

M. JACQUET'S HOUSE

The **University of Lille** occupies spacious buildings inaugurated in 1895. An important library and various wings have since been added, including the Coal and the Gosselet Geological and Mineralogical Museums, the Electro-Technical and Pasteur Institutes, etc. The University of Lille is the second in importance in France.

On the left, at the end of the Place Philippe le Bon, take the Rue Solférino which crosses the Place Jeanne d'Arc and leads to the Rue de Douai.

From the Place Philippe le Bon, the tourist may visit the **curious Monument** built by the Germans in the Southern Cemetery, where several thousands

THE UNIVERSITY

of their soldiers were buried. The monument represents a Walkyrie carrying off a dead warrior to the Walhalla (*p.* 64).

To reach the Cemetery, take the Rue des Pyramides, on the right of the Church, then the Rue des Postes, go through the Porte des Postes and follow the Rue du Faubourg des Postes to the cemetery. Return to the Porte des Postes, taking on the right the Boulevard Victor Hugo which leads back to the crossing of the Rue Solférino and the Boulevard des Écoles (*see Itinerary, p.* 36).

If preferred, the tourist can go direct from Philippe le Bon Square to the Douai Gate, via the Rue Solférino (*continued by the Rue de Douai*), *passing between the University and St. Michael's Church.*

CRATER CAUSED BY THE EXPLOSION

The "Dix-huit Ponts" (*see p. 23*)

On reaching the Rue de Douai, the cracked walls of the houses, many of them roofless, which were damaged by the **Explosion** of the **German Ammunition Depot** known as the "Dix-huit Ponts," come into view. The tourist will get a closer view of them as he proceeds. *At the Douai Gate, take the Boulevard de Belfort on the left,* which leads to the scene of the catastrophe. The **crater** is still plainly distinguishable, although its sides are no longer sharp, and grass is springing up everywhere.

Climb to the highest point of the fortifications above the crater, to get a good view of this moving scene.

To the right and left extends the regular and picturesque line of the Vauban fortifications, the red brick walls standing out well against the green of the grass-covered slopes. In the nearest walls are large crevices, while

SPINNING MILL DESTROYED BY THE EXPLOSION

THE RUE DE RONCHIN

below, the tourist sees the crater strewn with rubbish and portions of the vaulting. In front, the wrecked spinning-mills, of which only the chimneys remain standing, and the devastated streets (Rue de Ronchin, Rue de Trévise, etc.), form impressive silhouettes.

Return to the Douai Gate, in front of which traces on the ground mark the site of a block of buildings burnt down by the Germans in October, 1914, when they entered the town. *Take again the Rue de Douai, then the Boulevard des Écoles, following the latter to the Rue and Porte de Paris.*

To the right of the Rue de Paris, in the Boulevard Louis XIV, are the **School of Arts and Craft** and the **Pasteur Institute.**

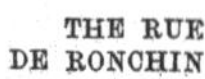

THE RUE DE RONCHIN

The Paris Gate

This gate was built in 1685-1695 from the plans of a local architect (Simon llant), to commemorate the return of Lille to France (1667). It s completely restored in 1895. The demolition of the old line of fortificans left this gate isolated in the middle of the town, and it was to ornament l finish off those portions which adjoined the ramparts that additions the same style were then made. The whole forms a Monumental Gate l Triumphal Arch.

In a large semi-circular arch is the Royal Coat of Arms, while below are Arms of Lille carved on a stone tablet. On either side of the latter are innels for receiving the drawbridge levers.

To the right and left, two Doric columns on pedestals support the whole the entablature with frieze and cornice, above which are trophies, helmets l flags. On pedestals between the columns are statues of Hercules *the right*) and Mars (*on the left*), while above are sculptured motifs in demief.

The most remarkable part of the monument is the great sculptured motif ich crowns the whole. In the middle, Victory seated amidst arms and ndards, raises her right hand to crown the King (Louis XIV), seen in the dallion immediately below. At Victory's feet, somewhat to the right l left, two figures of Fame proclaim the glory on trumpets.

The whole is expressive and graceful, attesting the great ability of the ist in treating this somewhat commonplace theme.

Take the Rue Carnot to the right of the Gate, skirting the Square Ruault, ich is the continuation, as far as the **Hospital of St. Saviour.**

This hospital, sometimes known as that of St. John the Evangelist, was

HOSPITAL OF SAINT-SAVIOUR *Door in one of the galleries*

founded in 1216, after the battle of Bouvines, by the Countess Jeanne de Constantinople. The present brick and stone buildings date from the 17th and 18th centuries.

In the Middle-Ages, hospital wards contained an altar at one end, so that the patients could hear Mass from their beds. A heavy curtain was then drawn, cutting off the altar from the remainder of the room.

In the hospital of St. Saviour, the choir of the chapel, which is lighted by high, broken-arch windows, still exists. A low, vaulted room, opening on the right, serves as an oratory for the nuns.

Skirting the Hospital on the right, the tourist comes to the **Noble Tower.**

Built in 1459, the Noble Tower was formerly the centre of the town's defences. It consisted originally of three stories, one of which contained ribbed Gothic vaulting. Of great size and massive construction, the tower is flanked by two smaller ones connected by a curtain. The upper portion of the tower has disappeared.

Near by is seen the steeple of the **church of St. Saviour,** a modern, pseudo-Byzantine edifice.

Return to the Paris Gate, via the Ruault Square, taking again the Rue de Paris. On the left, at No. 224, is a high gabled wall containing vestiges of a broken-arch bay, all that remains of the old **Hospice Ganthois,** founded in 1466 by *Jean de la Cambe,* surnamed Ganthois. The right wing was rebuilt in the 17th century. Over the entrance appears the date "1664." An interior court, shaped like a cloister, leads to the patients' ward.

THE NOBLE TOWER

THIRD ITINERARY

(*Follow the* **arrows** *along the streets indicated by* **continuous lines**).

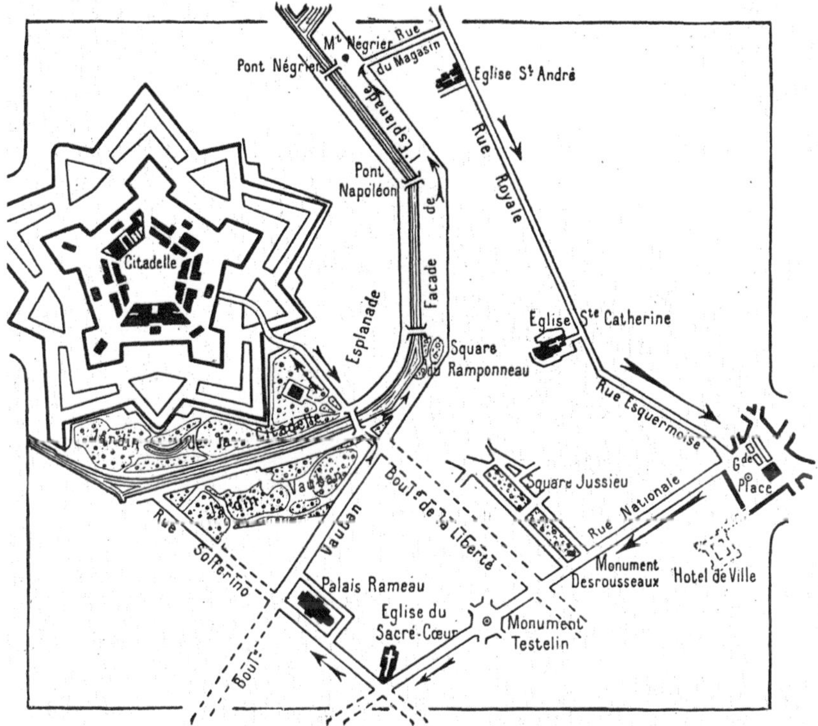

From the Grande Place to the Citadelle

Monuments to be seen on the way: The **Monument to Desrousseaux** in the Jussieu Square, the **Testelin Monument,** the **Church of the Sacred Heart,** the **Palais Rameau;** the **Bridges over the Deule, Monument to Negrier, Churches of St. André** and **St. Catherine.**

The temporary bridges mentioned further on, existed in April, 1919. In whatever state the tourist may find them, he need only *follow the Deule canal, after the* **Jardin Vauban,** *cross the first bridge he meets, and turn back to the left (if necessary) on the other side, until he comes to the avenue which opens out on the right opposite the Boulevard de la Liberté, and which leads to the* **Citadelle.**

Leave the Grande Place by the Rue Nationale, following the latter as far as the church of the Sacred Heart, whose high unfinished tower will be seen on the right. *To the right is the* **Jussieu Square** (landscape garden laid out by Barillet in the moats of the old fortifications), at the entrance to which is a **monument** to the local poet and song-writer **Desrousseaux**

MONUMENT TO DESROUSSEAUX.

(photo opposite), who started his career (1820-1892) as a simple working-man, and whose dialect songs are still sung. At the foot of the monument is the figure of a young mother rocking her child to sleep, recalling the composer's most popular song; "*Dors, min p'tit quinquin.*"

Cross the Boulevard de la Liberté, then skirt the **Testelin Monument.** *M. Testelin* was Prefect of the North of France and "Organizer of National Defence in the North in 1870-1871." The monument bears traces of the bombardment, while the bronze statues which surrounded the pedestal were carried away by the Germans.

On reaching the **Church of the Sacred Heart,** *turn to the right and follow the Rue de Solferino to the Boulevard Vauban, on the right of which is the* **Palais Rameau.**

The Palais Rameau

This fairly large building was erected in 1878, with the financial help of an agriculturist named *Rameau.* The principal hall is used for exhibitions, more especially horticultural. The rather **curious façade** includes a **bust of Rameau** flanked by figures of the goddesses Flora (flowers) and Pomona (fruits). In the rear of the Palace Garden is a fine circular **conservatory.**

THE PALAIS RAMEAU.

On leaving the Palais, take on the right the Boulevard Vauban which, a little further on, crosses the **Jardin Vauban** (pretty public garden), leading to the **Canal de la Moyenne Deule.**

Skirting a portion of the Citadelle and continuing the canal of the Haute Deule, this canal connects Lille with la Bassée and Douai. The river Deule was first opened up to navigation in 1271, while in 1830 its sidings were improved and the water-way deepened.

In April, 1919, it was necessary to follow the Deule as far as the Square du Ramponneau,

THE CITADELLE ROYAL GATE.

ere a temporary wooden bridge had been built close to a half-destroyed t-bridge. After crossing the bridge, visitors had to come back to the left far as the first avenue on the right leading to the Citadelle (*see p.* 49).

The Citadelle

This masterpiece of the fortification art is the work of Vauban (17th tury). In shape a regular pentagon, it includes numerous detached -works. Entrance to it is gained through the Royal Gate, which dates m 1670 (*photo above*). It contains barracks and a chapel (photo below), l it was in the latter that the hostages of Lille spent their nights during German occupation (*p.* 12).

Jacquet, Deconinck, Maertens, Verhulst and **Trulin** were shot in the thern moats by the Germans (*p.* 18).

After visiting the Citadelle, re-cross the bridge, turn to the left and follow **Façade de l'Esplanade,** *fine avenue planted with linden-trees, which runs ngside the canal.* The ruins of **Napoléon Bridge,** blown up by the re-ating Germans, *will be noticed* (*photo p.* 52).

Further on, at the northern end of the avenue, is the **Négrier Bridge,** ich was also destroyed by the Germans. Looking towards Napo-n Bridge, the **tower of St. Catherine's church** appears above the

THE CITADELLE CHAPEL.

NAPOLÉON BRIDGE (*January*, 1919).

NAPOLÉON BRIDGE *before destruction.*

The Napoléon Bridge dated from 1912. It was destroyed by the retreating Germans

Beyond the bridge is seen the tower of St. Catherine's Church (*see p.* 54)
This photograph was taken from the Négrier Bridge (*p.* 53)

NÉGRIER BRIDGE.

ees bordering the canal. Near by is the **statue of General Négrier** by a (1849), *photo below,* which was damaged by flying débris, when the idge was blown up.

Take the Rue du Magasin on the right to the Rue Royale, and follow the latter to : right. With its continuation, **the Rue Esquermoise,** which leads to the ande Place, the Rue Royale forms one of the main arteries of the old town.

The **Church of St. André** is reached shortly afterwards.

Church of Saint-André.

This church was erected in 1702. The doorway, with its two tall modern ,tues of St. Peter and St. Andrew in niches, is of two different orders, perposed and divided by an entablature, e whole being surmounted by a triangular liment.

Near the entrance are two **paintings:** e Purification, and The Adoration of e Wise Men, by *Otto Venius.* In the ithern aisle is a St. Theresa in Heaven *A. de Vuez*; in the chapel of St Joseph: d sending his Son to save the World, *Van Oost*; on the High Altar: Martyr- n of St. Andrew, by a local artist, *Descamps*; on either side of the choir, rble **busts** of St. Peter and St. Paul, by *ellin*; in the northern aisle, the Annun- tion, by *A. de Vuez*; in the Chapel of e Virgin, the Virgin giving the scapulary one Simon Stock, by *Jean Van Oost*; **ilver Tabernacle** with bas-relief repre- ting The Crucifixion, by the local gold- ith, *Baudoux*; an 18th century wrought- n **railing;** 16th century sacedotal **naments** from the Abbey of Loos. The **lpit** (*photo p.* 54) by *J.-B. Daneson* of lenciennes, dates from 1876. Its sound-

STATUE OF GENERAL NÉGRIER.

THE PULPIT, CHURCH OF ST. ANDRÉ.

ing-board represents a heavy curtain raised by an angel.

Further on in the Rue Royale, after the Banque de France, in a small street on the right, is the Church of St. Catherine (photo below).

Church of St. Catherine

Like many Flemish churches, that of St. Catherine has no transept, and consists of three practically identical naves. Standing out from the façade, a large square tower, flanked at the corners by eight buttresses, supports the ancient timber-work **belfry** — one of the finest in the region. The bell-chamber is lighted by broken-arch bays. One of the heavy bells (1403) bears a curious **inscription** in rhymes. Below the tower is the great doorway.

The exterior decoration is very sober in style. The right-hand side of the building is masked by houses. The left façade, between whose high mullioned windows are buttresses decorated with small ornamental arcades, has been restored in modern times. Belts of foliage run round the gutters of the roof. The carvings on the great and small doorways are modern.

Inside the church are two rows of columns on moulded bases, the corbels of whose capitals are ornamented with foliage. The nerves of the vaulting are plaster.

In the northern aisle is a **painting** by *Rubens*: The Martyrdom of St. Catherine, dating from about 1622; in the Chapel of Our Lady of Lourdes, on the left of the choir in a small niche, is a **statuette** of Our Lady of the Seven Afflictions, given by *Philippe le Bon*, in 1450, to the collegiate of St. Peter. In the Chapel of the Sacred Heart, to the right of the choir, is a small 15th century **funeral monument** in a niche. The **carved stalls** ornamented with statues are also noteworthy.

CHURCH OF ST. CATHERINE, *seen from the Rue Royale.*

After visiting the church return to the Rue Royale; at Nos. 1 and 3, **curious 17th century houses.**

At the end of the Rue Royale, take the Rue Esquermoise (which is the continuation, and which contains **18th century houses** at Nos. 83 and 101), *as far as the Grande Place.*

FOURTH ITINERARY

(*Follow the* **arrows** *along the streets indicated by* **continuous lines**)

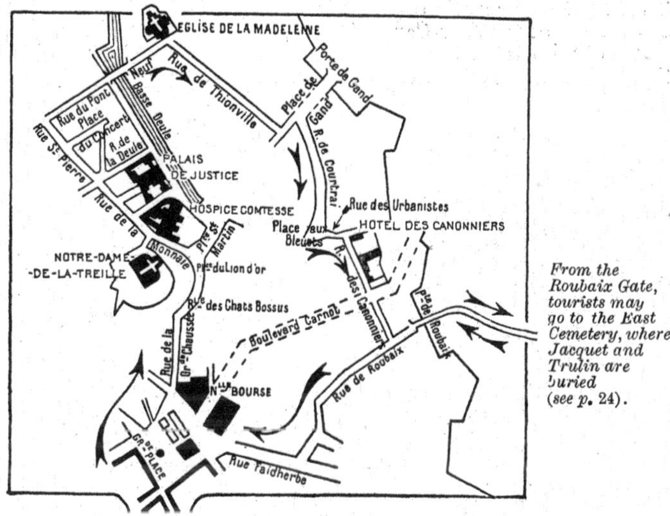

From the Roubaix Gate, tourists may go to the East Cemetery, where Jacquet and Trulin are buried (*see p.* 24).

THE OLD TOWN

Chief Buildings : The **Church of Our Lady of the Vine; Comtesse spital, Law Courts, Church of St. Magdalene, Hôtel des Canonniers, ubaix Gate.**

Starting from the Grande Place, cross the Place du Théâtre and take the e de la Grande Chaussée, on the left of the Nouvelle Bourse : 13th and 14th tury houses at Nos. 11, 14, 15, 42 and 52. *On the right take the Rue des its Bossus and Place du Lion d'or, leave the Place St. Martin on the right, l take the Rue de la Monnaie on the left.* At No. 31 in this street, opens a row passage leading to the **Church of Our Lady of the Vine,** which being erected on the site of the Castle of Buc. When finished, it will one of the largest of modern Gothic churches. The inhabitants of Lille re already surnamed it " the Cathedral." Building was begun in 1855, m plans by the English architects Clutton and Burges, revised by the uit, Arthur Martin. 13th century in style, the choir, over crypt, is only f-finished, while the remainder of the edifice has not yet been begun.

In the chapel of the apse, over the altar, is a **statue** of Our Lady of the ie, venerated since the 13th century as the Patron Saint of the town. a chapel on the left are **plans** and a **model in relief** of the finished silica.

Return to the Rue de la Monnaie, at No. 32 of which is the **Comtesse spital.**

The **Comtesse Hospital** was founded in 1243 by Countess Jeanne de Flandre; the entrance dates from 1649, and opens on to a curious vaulted passage. A 15th century gable faces the Rue Comtesse.

Inside are **paintings** by *Arnould de Vuez* and *Wamps*. The chapel contains fine **timber-work vaulting** and a **commemorative tablet** inscribed with the names of the French officers who died in this hospital of wounds received at the Battle of Fontenoy.

Follow the Rue de la Monnaie as far as the Place du Concert. Turn to the right as far as the Canal de la Basse Deule, by the side of which is the **Colonnade** of the Law Courts (1837) (*photo below*).

The Deule is an important river about 40 miles long, which traverses the whole of the coalfields of Northern France, and helps to carry the enormous

THE PALAIS DE JUSTICE AND THE PONT-NEUF

traffic connected with the metallurgical, cotton, woollen and sugar industries of that region.

Follow the Deule Quay to the left, to the steps of the Pont Neuf. (*If motoring or driving, the tourist will have to go via the Place du Concert, Rue St. André, then taking on the right the Rue du Pont Neuf.*) The latter crosses the Deule by the **Grand Pont** or **Pont Neuf,** formerly called the Pont Royal. Built in 1701 from plans by the architect Vollant, this bridge connects up the two parallel roads which run alongside the canal. Originally it was composed of six arches, two of which spanned the river, the other four passing over the low-level roads on either bank.

To allow the trams to pass, the two arches on the quay where the colonnade of the Palais de Justice stands have been replaced in recent times by an unartistic platform resting on iron pillars, which has spoilt the appearance of the bridge.

Steps connect the bridge with the quays.

After crossing the bridge, the tourist arrives in front of the **Church of St. Magdalene** (1675), a vast round edifice surrounded by chapels and surmounted by a cupola. It contains several interesting **paintings:** on the High Altar, the Resurrection of Lazarus, by *Jacques Van Oost*; under the dome, The Four Doctors of the Latin Church, by the same painter; in the Chapel of Our Lady of Help, The Adoration of the Shepherds, by

ST. MAGDALENE'S CHURCH.

bens; in the Chapel of the St. crement, Christ crucified, by *n Dyck*: at the entrance to the oir, The Woman of Samaria d the Canaanitish Woman, by *nould de Vuez.*

Follow the Rue de Thionville, ich begins opposite St. Maglene's Church, then turn to the into the Place de Gand, at the l of which is the **Gand Gate.** *the right take the Rue de Couri which leads to the Place aux uets. At the lower end of this are, turn to the left into the e des Urbanistes, then take the t street on the right, the Rue des nonniers, which skirts the* **Hôtel s Canonniers.** *The latter,* merly an Urbanist Convent, s given by NAPOLEON in 1804 the "Sedentary Gunners Corps" Lille. It contains town records d a small museum of local erest.

A little further on, at the corner of the Rue des Canonniers and the Rue Roubaix is the old **Hôtel d'Aigremont,** dating from the 18th century.

Turning to the left into the Rue de Roubaix, the tourist comes out in front the **Roubaix Gate.**

THE ROUBAIX GATE.

ROUBAIX GATE.

As in the case of the Tournai Gate (p. 34), the retreating Germans blew up the bridge over the moat, seen on p. 57 (before) and above (after) the explosion. A temporary road replaces the Bridge.

ROUBAIX GATE

The **Roubaix** or **St. Maurice Gate** dates from about 1620, and was erected from the plans of *Jean de Mesre, Jean Petit* and *Jean Fayet.* Of its three entrances, the middle one only is ancient. Above each entrance is carved a coat of arms. The one in the centre, forming a tympanum, is between two pilasters supporting a triangular pediment. At the top is a row of battlements, with a stone niche surmounted by a broken pediment in the centre. The niche contains the **statue** of a woman.

Over the passage is a slate-roofed building ornamented with coloured glazed bricks.

Go through the gate and take the Rue du Faubourg de Roubaix to the **Eastern Cemetery.** The graves of **Jacquet** and **Trulin** are in this cemetery (*see photos p.* 24).

Return to the Grande Place by the Rue de Roubaix, Rue des Ponts-de-Comines and Rue Faidherbe.

ROUBAIX-TOURCOING

From Lille to Roubaix and Tourcoing, via the Boulevard des Trois Villes.

Total Distance, including return journey: 16 miles.

ROUBAIX, one of France's **chief industrial centres,** is of very ancient gin. The first important mention of it in history, however, only goes k to the 15th century (1469), when one, *Peter of Roubaix,* obtained per- sion from Charles the Bald to manufacture cloth. It was occupied and ked several times by foreign invaders. In 1792 it was taken by the strians, in 1794 by the English, and in 1914 by the Germans.

In 1554, Roubaix, which had become a rival to Lille, obtained permission m Charles-Quint and later (1609) from the Council of the Arch-Dukes of stria, to manufacture velvet, fustian and common grey linen cloth.

A decree of the State Council in 1762, granting similar privileges to all parishes, was the subject of long lawsuits, which were decided against le.

The popular song-writer, *Gustave Nadaud* (1820-1893) was a native of ubaix.

There are no monuments in the town anterior to the Revolution.

The population, largely composed of the working classes, increased rapidly ween 1881 and 1891, and numbered 120,000 in 1914. The suburbs: ttrelos, Lys, Croix, Wasquehal and Mouvaux, are extensions of the town elf and are growing steadily.

Since 1830 Roubaix has been an important centre for **wool combing l spinning,** the machinery employed comprising 700 washing, carding, nbing and weaving machines and 300,000 spindles. Before the War, wool-spinning mills produced **6,000 tons** of yarn annually, the whole which was used in France.

The **dyeing** and **finishing** industries, which date back to 1760, had adily prospered. In 1914, 48 firms, employing 8,000 workpeople, were gaged in this branch.

TOURCOING shared the fate of Flanders during the course of its history. e English and Flemish burnt it during the 14th century, while the French zed it in 1477. In 1566-1568 it was twice sacked by the Gueux, and the ke of Albe held it to ransom. From 1667 to 1708 it was annexed to France Louis XIV. Later it fell successively under the yoke of the Austrians, tch and Saxons. On May 18th, 1794, the French beat the Duke of York's ops at Tourcoing, and paved the way for the Victory of Fleurus on ne 26th.

Tourcoing is essentially an **industrial town.** Its population has adily increased since 1491, when it numbered 2,500. In 1851 it had grown 27,615 and in 1914 to 82,644.

From time immemorial Tourcoing has been a **wool manufacturing** tre. Here, the wool is first washed and dried, then treated with cocoa- t fat, before combing, and lastly spun. Since 1845 the combing has been ne mechanically (Heilman's system). The same may be said of the spinning, ich, since 1811, was done on Bobo machines. Before the War, **5,000 ns** of spun wool were exported annually.

Among the **specialities** made at Tourcoing were: **fine thread, table- ths** and **tapestry-work** of mixed silk and mercerised cotton (well known their fine colouring and reasonable price), and **carpets** of the Wilton and iental types.

PANORAMA OF ROUBAIX (*Cliché LL.*)

ROUBAIX

Itinerary : *Leave Lille by the Boulevard Carnot at the Place du Théâtre, between the Theatre and the New Bourse. Follow the Boulevard des Trois Villes to* **Roubaix.** *Enter the latter by the Rue de Lille, follow its continuation, the Rue Neuve, which leads to the Grande Place :* **Hôtel de Ville** *and* **Church of St. Martin.**

Hôtel de Ville

The present building is the work of the architect *Laloux* (1911) ; it replaced the old Town Hall, built in 1845 and pulled down in 1907. The latter, as the town grew, had several times been enlarged and otherwise altered, but had finally become too small for a population of more than 50,000 workpeople and an annual production exceeding 500,000,000 frs. in value.

The new Town Hall is a fine building, with a **frieze** representing scenes

THE HÔTEL DE VILLE (*Cliché LL.*)

m the local industries. A wing on the right serves as the **Stock-Exchange,** ile another on the left contains the town's records.

Church of St. Martin

This church, which was rebuilt and transformed in 1849, recalls vaguely 15th century Gothic style of the original edifice. Only the **steeple** ancient. The church has five naves and contains four **ancient tombs** l a Flemish **altar-screen.**

Take the Rue de la Gare, to the Nord-West of the Grande Place. At the ner of the Rue Nain is the **National School of Industrial Arts,** to which

THE GRANDE PLACE AND CHURCH OF ST. MARTIN *(Cliché LL.)*

been added a **Museum** of **Paintings** and **Sculpture** (recently organized *M. Victor Champier*), a **Textile Museum** and a **Library** containing 000 volumes.

The School proper (whose courses, which are well attended, include dyeing, nning, weaving, etc.) and its annexes (museum and library) are installed a fine building erected in 1889 from the plans of the architect, *F. Dutert,* o designed the Galerie des Machines in Paris. Built of dressed stone l brick, the three doorways lead to the library, museums (sculpture, paint-s, art-history and textiles) and the public lecture-hall.

The **central pediment** by Allar, represents Industry and Art. On the **diments of the pavilions** are symbolized: The Arts (*by Lanson*) and Sciences (*by Hughes*). The **frieze** (by Laoust) represents, symbolically, various branches of learning taught in the school.

At the station, take the Rue de l'Alma on the right, then turn to the left into Rue de Tourcoing, which leads straight to **Tourcoing.**

THE GRANDE PLACE.

GERMAN HEAVY ARTILLERY CROSSING THE SQUARE

TOURCOING

The Rue de Roubaix (continuation of the Rue de Tourcoing) is prolonged by the Rue Carnot, which leads to the Grande Place. Here the tourist will find the **Church of St. Christopher.**

ST. CHRISTOPHER'S CHURCH (*Cliché LL.*)

THE DOOR-WAY (*Cliche LL.*)

THE GRANLE PLACE.

GERMAN REVIEW IN THE GRANDE PLACE

The Church of St. Christopher

The original church was erected in the 12th or 13th century, but was entirely rebuilt in 1860, in 15th century Gothic style. The body of brick and stone, with its various balustrades, graceful sculptured pinnacles, and richly decorated tracery windows, recalls the churches of that period, but it is evident from the aspect of the interior, where the decoration is less rich, that the church is modern. The spire above the tower is 17th century.

To the N.W. of the church is the **Hôtel de Ville,** a modern, French Renaissance building, surmounted by a large dome. It contains a **library** of about 10,000 volumes, a **museum** of fine **paintings,** mostly modern (*Paul Chabas, David, Guardi, Harpignies, Peter Naefs, Henri Zo, Henri Zuber*) and specimens of **old clothstuffs** of local manufacture.

GERMAN MONUMENT IN TOURCOING CEMETERY.

CONTENTS

GERMAN MONUMENT IN THE SOUTH CEMETERY, LILLE (*see p.* 44)

PRINTED IN GREAT BRITAIN BY WILLIAM CLOWES AND SONS, LIMITED, LONDON

X—2,114-6-19-25

www.ingramcontent.com/pod-product-compliance
Ingram Content Group UK Ltd.
Pitfield, Milton Keynes, MK11 3LW, UK
UKHW041845190726
13854UKWH00002B/716